WHAT OTHERS ARE SAYING

I finished reading your book today and found it a good overview of events as well as an interesting story about Isaac Levan. What was new to me was the whole concept of the redemption and subsequent indenture. I thought all indentures were planned before they left port, not upon arrival in America. So even I learned something! Good luck with it.

Paul

Paul R. Ackermann
Museum Specialist/Conservator
West Point Museum, Bldg 2110
United States Military Academy
West Point NY, 10996-2001
845-938-7338/2203 TEL
845-938-7478 FAX

This book is based on the life and service of Isaac Levan, a patriot of the American Revolution, whose journey is both compelling and revolting at the same time. The insights into the American Revolution by the author, are pivotal in understanding facets of this war, but the story of Levan reveals the oftentimes invidiousness of man's nature and the relentless cruelty of life's setbacks. The reader will find this book absorbing as Isaac Levan, provokes great honor and even greater pity. An elucidating and stirring read.

Patricia Markus
Literary Editor
Buford, GA

EIGHT YEARS
A SOLDIER

EIGHT YEARS
A SOLDIER

RON JONES

To Jack
Thank you for your
interest in this rich
period of our American
history.
Best Wishes

TATE PUBLISHING
AND ENTERPRISES, LLC

Published by Tate Publishing & Enterprises, LLC
127 E. Trade Center Terrace | Mustang, Oklahoma 73064 USA
1.888.361.9473 | www.tatepublishing.com

Tate Publishing is committed to excellence in the publishing industry. The company reflects the philosophy established by the founders, based on Psalm 68:11,

"The Lord gave the word and great was the company of those who published it."

Book design copyright © 2016 by Tate Publishing, LLC. All rights reserved.
Cover design by Maria Louella Mancao
Interior design by Manolito Bastasa

Published in the United States of America
ISBN: 978-1-68207-771-9
Biography & Autobiography / Military
15.11.10

This book is dedicated to my wife, Annette, without whose urging, encouragement, and support, this would never have been possible.

To my son, Philip, who I hope one day will pass along to his family the rich history of our ancestors.

To the memory of my father, Hebron Edward Jones, who served his country honorably in the United States Marine Corps. My mother, Josephine Manes Jones, and their ancestors who served honorably in the war for American independence.

I am forever grateful to my cousin, Patricia Markus, for her invaluable assistance in proofreading my work and correcting my many grammatical errors

I am also indebted to Mr. Paul Ackerman, museum specialist/conservator, of the West Point Museum for his assistance with historical data.

Pictures of revolutionary figures are courtesy of Wikipedia.

Cover painting *Dawn of the Regiment* with permission from the artist, Rick Reeve, to whom I am greatly indebted.

CONTENTS

Part I
Declaration

Part II
The Provost Guard

Part III
Exhibit I

FOREWORD

THE INSPIRATION FOR this novel comes from a declaration made by Isaac Levan, a soldier in the Continental Army during the war for American independence. He made his declaration on January 24, 1837, before the Court of Burke County, North Carolina.

This declaration and the correspondence that followed over the next ten years or so came to my attention while researching my family genealogy and the involvement of my ancestors during this formative period of our nation's history.

The declaration struck me as one of the most fascinating documents I've ever read. It quite simply describes the service of a revolutionary soldier who served his country uninterruptedly for eight years and three months.

My interest was of both a historical and personal nature: historical, because I have a great interest in history and especially the formation of our country and personal, because I thought this man might be my fourth great-grandfather. I felt it was possible that I might have a family connection to Isaac Levan because of his life after the Revolution.

Two years after the war, in 1785, Levan left his home in Berks County, Pennsylvania, and moved to the Catawba River area, of North Carolina. He is enumerated in the 1790 census of Lincoln County, where he continues to be found until 1850 when he is listed in a home for the poor in adjoining Catawba County.

This region was heavily settled by people of German ancestry who migrated there from the Philadelphia area during the years after the war. Many of these families later moved to the Cumberland Plateau, east of Nashville, Tennessee. It is due to the relocation to Tennessee, that I suspected a familial connection to Isaac Levan. I had originally thought that he may have been the father of my third great-grandfather James Benjamin Levan, who settled in White County, Tennessee just after 1800. This is evidenced by the appearance of his name with those who signed the petition to form Warren County, Tennessee, out of that portion of White County in 1806. In addition, many of the German families who moved from North Carolina to Tennessee appear on the early censuses of Warren County, including the family of Benjamin Levan, as his name is always listed. This initially seemed a strong indication that those families who relocated as a group from Pennsylvania did the same in their movement to Tennessee. Adding to the speculation was a family history of Isaac Levan, which indicated that he had a son named Benjamin. However, additional research suggested that it was unlikely that Isaac Levan would have had a son old enough to have been of the age to have signed a petition, such as the one my ancestor signed in 1806.

Regardless of a possible family connection, I felt this man's story needed to be told, as it documents, as few accounts do, a soldier's story for the entire eight years of the American Revolution. This included the period between Cornwallis's surrender and the formal peace agreement of 1783. Many high-ranking officers served for the entire war; however, it is virtually unheard of for a soldier, who apparently never rose above the rank of private, to have remained committed to service for such an extended period. Many enlistments were for a period of a few months or a year and upon fulfilling their obligation most men returned to their homes. It was because of Levan's unique situation, which will be addressed later in the book, that he remained so committed.

While recounting Isaac Levan's wartime experiences, with his declaration as a historical outline, I have added fictionalized dialogue and accounts to personalize these experiences and to hopefully tell a story which will make enjoyable and educational reading.

Isaac Levan's story begins in Germany, in the spring of 1773. His exact date of birth is unknown, as the only documents bearing his age are in conflict. The Federal Census Mortality Schedule records his death in January 1850 and lists his age as ninety-six. The Federal Census, taken the same month, lists the same age, suggesting that he was born about 1753. This information is contradicted by his declaration for pension made January 24, 1837, which indicated his age at "near seventy-nine." Later correspondence regarding his pension request would state that he was sixteen when he arrived in America. These statements indicate that he was likely born in 1756 or 1757. It is certain that he was at least sixteen, as records indicate he signed the oath of allegiance to the king upon his arrival, which was required by law of all men sixteen and older.

Regardless of his year of birth, it is evident Isaac Levan came to the Colonies as a young man still in his teens. That he came alone is substantiated by the names on the ship's list and of the immigration and indenture records of Philadelphia in the late summer of 1773. It is also likely, based on statements made by Levan himself, and from statistical information taken on literacy, during this period of German history, that young Levan was capable of reading and writing in his native German.

His reasons for taking this bold step are also unknown but are very likely due to the various socioeconomic factors existing in his German homeland in the mid eighteenth century. Poverty, a leading reason for much of the immigration, was widespread in central Germany and resulted from a number of factors. Among these were the devastation created by wars between the German states and meager harvests resulting from both poor lands and drought. Other factors included governmental oppression, high taxes, and religious persecution and in some cases inheritance laws favoring the eldest son, by prohibiting the division of property, leaving younger sons and daughters to look elsewhere for subsistence.

Each of these factors, especially the agricultural failures, led to increased internal migration from farms to the larger cities of Germany. This compounded the issue of poverty and disease and consequently led to an increase in external immigration to the British Colonies and to a lesser degree other locations. The exodus to America had begun in the 1680s, had continued with the Palatine immigration of the early 1700s, and expanded significantly from 1727 until 1769, with the peak years being in the early 1750s.

As with many other young German men and women searching for a way to better the prospects of their life, Isaac Levan, likely came in contact with a group of people who have come to be called soul vendors. These unscrupulous cohorts, of notorious slave agents, deceived hundreds of young Germans hungry for adventure or simply desperate to make a better life for themselves. Eager to believe the stories of riches in the East Indies or the English Colonies in America, they were easy prey for these worldly artists of deception. Their newly found "friends" often pretended to hail from the same region or German state and easily convinced these naïve refugees that they too were concerned for their welfare. These flesh peddlers would offer to secure for them passage to their desired location on a ship captained by an acquaintance or friend. They would then ply them with food and drink before delivering them to the agents for whom they worked in the Dutch cities of Amsterdam and Rotterdam. It was here many would begin their journey to their destination in the new world.

Two personal accounts have survived from young immigrants who became shipmates of Isaac Levan. Johann Carl Buettner and John Frederick Whitehead, whose surname is recorded in the ship's list as that of his stepfather, Kukuck, both wrote of the experiences that brought them to be "sold into slavery" and of the hardships they witnessed and endured on their voyage. The experiences related in these two narratives are very similar, with Whitehead writing in much more detail of his experiences aboard ship.

I have drawn from the writings of both of these men in order to present a factual representation of the conditions under which early immigrants came to America.

INTRODUCTION

INNUMERABLE CHARACTERS HAVE played roles in the drama that is our American history. Some have left footprints never to be erased by the sands of time. Others have played out their parts in stark anonymity and have disappeared without any record of their participation in this drama nor mention of how each, in their own way, may have contributed to the incredible story that is America's.

During the years between what has been called the Boston Massacre in 1770, the ratification of the United States Constitution in 1787 and the election of George Washington as the first president in 1789, many made significant contributions to the formation of the first republican form of government on the globe.

Those included in this introduction are but a few of those who participated in some way in the formation of the new nation. Some laid down their lives, many gave up fortunes, two would later become traitors to the American cause, and others became the leaders who would direct the United States into the nineteenth century. All were important players in the American story no matter how insignificant their role, on history's stage, seemed to be at the time.

My Ancestors

Archibald E. Burden, my fifth great-grandfather, was born in 1745 in Amherst County, Virginia, and died in 1806 in Elbert County, Georgia. He served in the Amherst County Militia, in 1778. DAR A017106

Isaac David, my fifth great-grandfather, was born May 30, 1756, in Cumberland County, Virginia, and died April 17, 1840, in Madison County, Georgia. He served as a private in the Virginia Militia from Henry County, under the command of Captain Critz. They served under General Greene at Guilford's Court House and took part in the battle there on March 25, 1781. The Company was later at Eutaw Springs, South Carolina, and the surrender at Yorktown, on October 19, 1781. DAR A030035

Peter David, my sixth great-grandfather, was born October 8, 1710, in the Parish of St. Martins, London, England. He died in 1781 in Henry County, Virginia. He served as Quartermaster, in the 14th Regiment of Foot, in the Continental Army, during 1777 and at Valley Forge in 1778. DAR A030042

James Davidson, my fourth great-grandfather, was born in Virginia, about 1750 and died in Scott County, Virginia, in 1826. He served in Captain James Thompson's Militia from Fincastle County during Lord Dunmore's War, and in 1781 accompanied Colonel William Campbell as part of the Over Mountain Men to Kings Mountain, a pivotal battle in the Revolution. DAR A131288

John Hancher, my fourth great-grandfather, was born in the mid 1730s in either Pennsylvania, or Frederick County, Virginia, and died in 1793 in Berkley County, Virginia. He served in the 12th, 8th and 4th Regiments of the Virginia Continental Line, from March 1777 until March 1779, seeing action at the battles of Brandywine, Germantown, and White Marsh and was with George Washington at Valley Forge. DAR A053911

Francis Power, my fifth great-grandfather, was born February 21, 1756, in Maryland, and died before August 3, 1818, in Madison County, Georgia. He enlisted January 3, 1776, in the 3rd Company, 14th Regiment, under Colonel John Glover, Esq. He also had service in the Company of Militia, from Bedford County, Virginia, under Captain Adam Clements in North Carolina, in May 1781. DAR A206216

Jacob Slagle (Schlegel) Sr., my third great-grandfather, was born June 10, 1723, in Lancaster, Pennsylvania, and died before April 9, 1790, in Berwick Township, York, Pennsylvania. He provided patriotic service to the Revolution. DAR A104987

Robert Tate Jr., my fourth great-grandfather, was born about 1745 in what then was Augusta County, Virginia, and died July 24, 1806, at Moccasin Creek, Russell County, Virginia. He served in Captain James Thompson's Militia from Fincastle, County, during Lord Dunmore's War and in 1781 accompanied Colonel William Campbell, as part of the Over Mountain Men to Kings Mountain, a pivotal battle in the Revolution. DAR A112164

James Vaughn, my fifth great-grandfather was born about 1745 in Southern Virginia, in what was then Brunswick County, and died in 1796 in Oglethorpe County, Georgia. He was the son-in-law of my 6th Great-Grandparents James and Arabella Wilkins. On February 19, 1776, he enlisted for two years in the 4th Virginia Regiment of the Continental Army, serving in Captain John Brent's Company, commanded by Colonel Robert Lawson and in Captain Jason Riddick Company, commanded by Colonel Thomas Elliott. The 4th Virginia Regiment, joined

George Washington's Army late in 1776 and Vaughn participated in the winter battles of Trenton and Princeton. In the fall
of 1777, James was with the army at the battles at Brandywine,
Germantown, and White Marsh before spending the winter of
1778 at Valley Forge, Pennsylvania. James was discharged on
February 19, 1778, after his two-year enlistment was complete.
DAR A204089

Arabella Smith Wilkins, my sixth great-grandmother, was
born circa 1721. She was the daughter of Luke Smith and
Arabella Gromarrin. She is recognized as a Revolutionary
Patriot, for providing support to the Revolution, as evidenced
by the Virginia Revolutionary War Public Service Claims.
DAR A203057

James Wilkins, my sixth great-grandfather, was born bout
1730 in Lunenburg County, Virginia. He died before October
8, 1781, in Mecklenburg County, Virginia. He was a captain
in the Virginia Militia, Mecklenburg First Battalion, and also
provided patriotic service to the Revolution. DAR A204089

Isaac Levan

Isaac Levan was born in Germany about 1757. He immigrated to America in the summer of 1773 arriving in Philadelphia on August 23, aboard the ship *Sally*. Unable to pay for his passage, he became indentured for a period of seven years to Mr. William Boyes, who had paid the 27.13 pound debt.

Eager for adventure and to be released from servitude, he joined the American cause against Great Britain in March 1775. His remarkable experience in the service of his adopted country is the subject of this book.

He lived the life of a soldier uninterruptedly for over eight years. He was a witness to many of the significant battles taking place in the Northeast and was on hand for the siege at Yorktown, which effectively ended the Revolution. During that time, he was to know hunger, lack of proper clothing and footwear, and other hardships often known only by men who choose to serve their countries.

Despite the many adversities he faced during the eight-plus years, each time he was discharged, he reenlisted for another three-year period. His lack of family in his adopted country is likely the reason for his continuing to serve throughout the war.

Levan's service includes participation in the following battles and campaigns:

- The capture of Ticonderoga and Crown Point
- The Canadian Campaign and the Battle of Quebec
- Brandywine
- Germantown
- White Marsh
- Monmouth Court House
- Stony Point
- Connecticut Farms
- Yorktown
- Other smaller skirmishes

General Benedict Arnold

Benedict Arnold was born January 14, 1741, in Norwich, Connecticut, to a very prominent New England family. His great-grandfather Benedict was an early governor of the Colony of Rhode Island and his father Benedict III, a successful businessman. His mother was the third great-granddaughter of Reverend John Lothrop whose descendants include six presidents of the United States. When war broke out between the American Colonies and Great Britain, Arnold, who had been a member of the Sons of Liberty, and as a teenager had served with the British against the French in the French and Indian War, was quickly drawn into the revolution serving initially as a captain of militia. He quickly demonstrated through his actions that he was both intelligent and brave.

Soon after the battles at Lexington and Concord, his company of Connecticut militia marched north to join the siege of Boston. Arnold, having some knowledge of the forts along the Hudson River, convinced leaders of the Massachusetts Committee of Safety to support a movement on Fort Ticonderoga, which he understood to be manned by only a few British troops. He was given the rank of colonel, and on May 3, 1775, he left to join ranks with Ethan Allen in Vermont and begin the movement toward Fort Ticonderoga.

After the capture of Fort Ticonderoga, men under Arnold captured Crown Point, which he used as a base for operations against the British on Lake Champlain and they made a daring raid on Fort St. Jean on the upper end of the Lake. Here, he seized supplies and a British sloop, which had just been completed at the shipyards there.

When the Continental Congress approved a movement on Quebec, he was given a colonel's commission in the Continental Army and was sent north with a force to join General Richard Montgomery in the assault. During that failed attack, Montgomery was killed and Arnold was wounded in the leg. Promoted to general, he continued to besiege Quebec until he was replaced and given responsibility for the city of Montreal as military commander.

After recovering from his wound, he returned to service and was again wounded in the left leg at the Battle of Ridgefield in Connecticut, after which he was promoted to major general, a rank he felt long overdue. He would go on to distinguish himself at the battles of Saratoga, where he was wounded in the same leg for the third time. This last wound forced him to leave active service, and it required several months of recuperation during which the second phase of his checkered history would unfold.

Appointed military commander of Philadelphia, he soon was drawn into the social scene of Philadelphia, where he became acquainted with influential citizens whose sympathies rested with Great Britain. He became bitter at the Continental Congress, for what he felt was their failure to compensate him properly for his service and to reimburse him for personal funds he had used to support the revolution. He began to focus his attentions on ways to increase his personal fortune. Despite continuing support from George Washington, he grew more and more bitter and obsessed with personal wealth until he was drawn into a plot to surrender the fortress at West Point, which had been placed under his command in 1780. The plan was foiled and led to the capture and execution of John Andre, the British officer with whom he had conspired.

Arnold managed to escape capture and joined the British Army with the rank of brigadier general. He served in that capacity until the fall of Yorktown in October of 1781 after which he left America for England.

During the remaining years of his life, he lived in both England and Canada. Seemingly always embroiled in controversy, he died in England in 1801 at the age of sixty. He was buried without military honors.

It is ironic that despite his early efforts to help win independence for what would become the United States, he is best known for his betrayal of his country. The name Benedict Arnold was afterward to become synonymous with the term *traitor*.

General Moses Hazen

Moses Hazen was born June 1, 1733, in Haverhill, Massachusetts. In his early twenties, he enlisted in an American colonial unit during the French and Indian War. He served in ranger groups with distinction, was commissioned first lieutenant, and promoted captain after leading a raid which captured Joseph Godin, who was a leader in inflaming the Indians against the British.

Volunteering himself and his men for numerous dangerous expeditions into the countryside around Quebec, he was wounded badly at the battle of Sainte-Foy in April 1760 and was forced to give up his ranger company. In 1761, because of the bravery he had exhibited, Hazen was allowed to purchase a lieutenant's commission in the 44th Regiment of Foot, in the British Army. He served in the 44th regiment as it performed garrison duty at Montreal until retiring on half pay, when it was reduced to nine companies in 1763.

Hazen settled in Montreal after the war, involving himself in various business ventures. When war erupted in 1775 between Britain and the American Colonies to the south, he was recommended for a commission by Governor Guy Carleton. Because his lands lay along a potential invasion route by the colonist, he felt required to decide between the two combatants, eventually siding with the colonist.

Hazen joined the Americans in the siege of Quebec, and after the siege had failed, he was dispatched to the Continental Congress at Philadelphia, bearing the news of the failure, news of the death of the American Commander Richard Montgomery, and a request for reinforcements. Two Canadian regiments of 1,000 men each were authorized by Congress with Hazen offered the command of one, with the rank of colonel and the second given to General Livingston. Recruitment was difficult and Hazen's regiment was eventually supplemented by Americans and is commonly referred to as Congress' Own.

Hazen commanded his regiment throughout the revolution; it saw action at Staten Island, New York, Brandywine, Germantown, and later Yorktown before being furloughed in July 1783 and disbanded in November of that same year.

Having lost everything during the war, Hazen lobbied Congress for compensation with little success. He spent his last twenty years in debt, often being sued and at times suing others. He was arrested several times for debt in his later years and died deeply in debt in February 1803.

General Charles Lee

Charles Lee was born February 6, 1732, in Cheshire, England. He attended school in Switzerland, mastering several languages. He began a career in the military at the early age of fourteen when his father, a colonel in the British army, purchased a commission for him as an ensign in the same regiment.

After completing his education, he joined his regiment, purchased a lieutenant's commission and was sent with the regiment to America in 1754 for service in the French and Indian War. While in America, he married the daughter of a Mohawk Indian chief and was known to the Mohawks as Ounewaterika or Boiling Water.

In 1756, Lee purchased a captain's commission in his regiment and continued to serve in the colonies until returning to Europe in 1760. Upon his return, his regiment was disbanded and he was retired as a major. He later served in the armies of Portugal and Poland. Returning to England after his adventures in Europe in the early 1770s, he found himself sympathetic to the American colonists in their differences with Britain, eventually immigrating to the area of Virginia, now part of West Virginia.

At the outset of war, he volunteered his services to the colonies, expecting because of his military experience to be named commander in chief of the Continental Army. His personal habits and demand for compensation worked against him and he was passed over for Washington who was of more steady character and who offered to serve without pay, asking only that his expenses be covered. Lee, however, often served as second in command, although Artemas Ward, who was not in good health, officially held the position. Unhappy at being rejected, Lee worked almost continually to undermine Washington and have him replaced.

In late 1776, as Washington retreated from New York to safety across the Delaware River, Lee was ordered to follow closely behind. Instead, while delaying his movement, he continued to write letters to various Congress members, seeking their support against Washington. As he continued to slowly follow the main army, Lee and a dozen of his guards stopped for a night's rest at White's Tavern in Basking Ridge, New Jersey, a short distance from his main force. Upon arising the next morning, while writing letters in his bedclothes, he was captured by a British patrol of two dozen mounted soldiers. Lee was held captive until exchanged in July 1777 during which time, he was treated more like a guest than a prisoner by the British.

At the Battle of Monmouth, Washington reluctantly chose Lee to lead an assault on the British as he was the most senior of his generals. Lee was ordered to attack the retreating enemy, but instead ordered his own forces to retreat. Retreating directly into Washington and his advancing troops, Lee was publicly reprimanded by Washington to which he responded with inappropriate language, was arrested for insubordination, and shortly thereafter court-martialed. Found guilty, he was relieved of command for one year. When attempts to have the court-martial's verdict overturned failed, he began open attacks on Washington's character.

These attacks only caused a further decline in Lee's popularity and he was challenged to a duel by Colonel John Laurens, an aide to Washington. Lee was wounded in the duel, and when recovered, he was released from his duty in January 1780. He subsequently retired to Philadelphia, Pennsylvania, where he died two years later in 1782.

In 1857, a plan for British military operations against the Americans was found in the family archives of British General Sir William Howe. The plan in Lee's handwriting was drafted in March 1777, while Lee was held prisoner by the British and under a threat of being tried as a deserter from the British Army, a threat resulting from the timing of the resignation of his British commission and his acceptance of an American commission.

Friedrich Wilhelm von Steuben

Commonly referred to as the Baron von Steuben, he was born on September 17, 1730, into a military family. His early years were spent in Russia, but his father returned to Germany when he was ten. By seventeen, he was an officer in the Prussian army, serving primarily in staff positions including that of Frederick the Great's headquarters. This service prepared him extraordinarily well for the primary duty he was to later serve in the American Revolution.

After having been discharged from his commission in the Prussian Army, he unsuccessfully sought positions in other European armies and, in the summer of 1777, was introduced to Benjamin Franklin in Paris. Franklin provided him with a letter of introduction and he soon left for America arriving in the fall of 1777. Presented to Congress, he offered to volunteer, without pay in the service of the Continental Army. Accepted and recommended by the Congress, Von Steuben reported for duty to General Washington at Valley Forge. He did not speak English, but his French was such that he could communicate with some of the French-speaking American officers. While at Valley Forge, he first worked with a small core group who then trained others until the whole army had received the instruction. The discipline he helped bring to the army was first displayed at the Battle of Monmouth. Here Washington's Army conducted itself in a professional manner the British had never before seen, standing toe to toe in a major battle with the best army in the world and at days end holding the field. He later served as both inspector general and major general of the Continental Army and in the final years of the war served as chief of staff to Washington. He is credited with writing the drill manual that became the standard for the United States Military until the War of 1812. After the war, Von Steuben lived in New York City and Utica, New York, where he died November 28, 1794.

Captain Bartholomew Von Heer

Born in Germany around 1730, Bartholomew Von Heer immigrated to the American colonies in 1775 at the recommendation of a countryman Frederick Weisenfels, then serving as a colonel, in the American Army. Von Heer had most recently been in Spain, where he had served in the Spanish Army, one of three European States whose military he had served. He is said to have been decorated for his service at the Battle of Zorndorf in August of 1758 during the Seven Years War, while in the service of Frederick of Prussia, and he was later in the French Army before his serving in the military in Spain.

He entered the American Military in 1775 as the adjutant of Colonel Livingston's Canadian Regiment. He served in that capacity until March of 1777 when he was appointed captain of one of the three companies in the Pennsylvania State Artillery regiment under the command of Colonel Thomas Proctor. This unit was eventually transformed into the 4th Continental Artillery. He continued in that capacity until June 1, 1778, at which time he was named by General George Washington to form a company of light dragoons, which were to become Von Heer's Provost Corps.

The Provost Company had developed as a result of correspondence between the two men which had begun the year before. In November 1777, he wrote General Washington, who he heard had expressed an interest in a permanent reorganized Provost Corp, or Marechausee, as it was known in Europe, within the Continental Army. He informed Washington in the letter that he had experience in both the horse and infantry in the armies of Europe and that he was familiar with the Marechausee and its duties and could train such a force for the Continental Army. Washington was intrigued by Von Heer's recommendations, and in January of the next year, he strongly suggested to Congress that a major reorganization of the Continental Army was required and that a Provost Corps should be established at that time. At his suggestion, Congress passed a resolution to form the Provost Corps on May 20, and on June 6, 1778, orders issued for the formation of this new Corps.

Von Heer recruited his new command from among German troops serving in Pennsylvania companies.

When finally assembled, the newly formed guard was almost entirely German, with many only speaking their native tongue. The ethnic makeup of the recruits proved to be beneficial as it was successful in forming a more cohesive unit. Once recruited, outfitted, and trained, the American Marechausee performed its duties with Von Heer as its commander, until 1783 when it was disbanded. After the war, Von Heer settled near Reading, Pennsylvania, where he died about 1790.

General Anthony Wayne

Anthony Wayne was born January 1, 1745, in Chester, County, Pennsylvania, near Valley Forge.

During his early adult years, he was a surveyor, a farmer, and served in several legislative positions in Pennsylvania.

At the onset of the war in 1775, he raised a militia and, in 1776, became colonel of the 4th Pennsylvania Regiment. He and his regiment were part of the Continental Army's unsuccessful invasion of Canada, where he was sent to aid Benedict Arnold. Following the failure at Quebec, he commanded a successful rear-guard action, at the Battle of Trois-Rivières. His service and fiery personality quickly earned him a promotion to the rank of Brigadier General on February 21, 1777, and would later bring the sobriquet of Mad Anthony.

He later commanded the Pennsylvania Line at Brandywine, Paoli, and Germantown and during the winter at Valley Forge, along with Nathaniel Greene, he took on the task of supplying and equipping the Continental Army as it redeveloped during the early months of 1778. After leaving winter quarters at Valley Forge, he led the American attack at the Battle of Monmouth. At Monmouth, his forces were pinned down by a numerically superior British force but held out until they were relieved by reinforcements sent by General George Washington. This scenario would play out again years later in the Southern campaign.

The highlight of his Revolutionary War service was very likely his victory at Stony Point. In July 1779, Washington named him to command the Corps of Light Infantry, a temporary unit of four regiments of light infantry companies from all the regiments in the Main Army. On July 16, 1779, in a bayonets-only night attack lasting just thirty minutes, three columns of the light infantry, stormed British fortifications at Stony Point, a cliffside redoubt commanding the southern Hudson River. The main attack was led personally by Wayne. The success of this operation provided a boost to the morale of an army which had at that time suffered a series of military defeats. For this victory, he was awarded a medal by the Continental Congress.

Subsequent successes, at West Point, and Green Spring in Virginia, increased his popular reputation as a bold commander. After the British surrendered at Yorktown, he went farther south and severed the British alliance with Native American tribes in Georgia. He then negotiated peace treaties with both the Creek and the Cherokee Indians for which Georgia rewarded him with the gift of a large rice plantation. He was promoted to major general on October 10, 1783.

After the war, he returned to Pennsylvania and served in the state legislature for a year in 1784. He then moved to Georgia and settled upon the tract of land granted him by that state for his military career. He was a delegate to the state convention which ratified the Constitution in 1788.

In his later years, at the request of President George Washington, he led an expedition in the Northwest Indian War, in territory ceded by Great Britain, to the United States, in the Treaty of Paris that had formally ended the conflict. Although now part of the United States, the natives living on the ceded land resisted annexation and, with assistance from the British, rebelled.

On August 20, 1794, his forces defeated the Indian confederacy at the Battle of Fallen Timbers, a decisive victory, which ended the war. Wayne then negotiated the Treaty of Greenville, between the tribal confederacy and the United States, which was signed on August 3, 1795. The treaty gave most of what is now Ohio, to the United States, and cleared the way for that state to enter the Union in 1803. Wayne died of complications from gout in 1796.

General Nathanael Greene

Nathanael Greene was born in Potowomut, Rhode Island, on August 7, 1742, to one of the oldest families in that colony. He knew the value of education but received little formal education himself. He educated himself with special emphasis on mathematics, law and the Bible, which was to form the core of his life beliefs and helped to establish the first public school in Coventry. Included in his library were books on military science, which he himself studied. The Quaker community to which he belonged objected to his interest in the military, but when he held firm to his convictions, the committee which had been called to investigate him dropped their inquiry. When hostilities began between the people of Massachusetts and Great Britain, he quickly went to Boston to offer his service as a private in the militia. From this humble military beginning, he was to rise to become General George Washington's most gifted and dependable officer. On May 8, 1775, the General Assembly of Rhode Island ordered that a force of 1,600 men be raised and entered into service as the Rhode Island Army of Observation. He was chosen as commander and promoted from private to brigadier general. A little over a month later, on June 22, 1775, he was appointed a brigadier general in the Continental Army by the Continental Congress. When Washington arrived in Boston, he was greeted by Greene and the two men quickly developed a lasting friendship. Recognizing his dependability, Washington assigned him

to the command of the city of Boston after the British withdrawal in March 1776.

He served Washington faithfully over the next two difficult years, and when providing supplies for the troops became
difficult during the winter at Valley Forge, the commanding
general beseeched Greene to accept the office of quartermaster general. He agreed, on the understanding that he should
retain the right to command troops in the field. With the help
of Anthony Wayne, the two reversed the fortunes of the troops
during that winter and rations and military supplies began to
flow into the camp.

When the American army broke camp in June of 1778 and
began their pursuit of the British who were returning by land
to New York, Greene was in command of the right wing of the
army at Monmouth on June 28, 1778. He continued as both a
field commander and as quartermaster general until in August
1780, after struggling with Congress over provisioning the
army, he resigned the latter office.

By that same summer, the war, which had seen its focus
moved to the South, was going badly for the Americans. The
generals, chosen by Congress, to command the Southern armies
had all failed miserably, and it was clear that new leadership was
necessary. The final blow, after the loss of both Savannah and
Charles Town, was the defeat at Camden, South Carolina, that
same summer in which the American troops broke and ran in
total disorder. The defeat at Camden left the Southern Army in
complete chaos. Cornwallis was now free to gather Southern
loyalists and bring the war to Virginia. Congress quickly moved
to provide the leadership believed necessary and entrusted the
choice to Washington, who lost no time in appointing his trusty
friend Nathanael Greene to the post. He wrote to Greene,

now at West Point, informing him of his decision. Although his forces were weak, badly equipped, and opposed by a superior force, he quickly developed a strategic plan to divide his army forcing Cornwallis to do the same. This strategy led to an extraordinary victory at Cowpens, South Carolina, on January 17, 1781. This victory essentially destroyed the second of two mounted armies, mostly loyalist, which Cornwallis had sent against the American forces in the western Carolinas. Victory at the Cowpens was quickly followed by another disaster for Cornwallis, at Guilford Courthouse, (present-day Greensboro, North Carolina) who was forced to retreat toward Wilmington and later to Yorktown in Virginia. There he was surrounded and forced to surrender his army, effectively ending the war. Greene meanwhile set about retaking the Carolinas, forcing the British back to Charles Town where they were contained until war's end. He returned home to Rhode Island after the war's conclusion but stayed only briefly. Having been granted large tracts of land for his service in the South, much of which he used to pay off debts incurred during the war, he moved in 1785 to Mulberry Grove, near Savannah. He twice declined the post of secretary of war, and on June 19, 1786, after suffering from heat stroke, Nathanael Greene died at the early age of forty-three.

The Marquis De Lafayette

Lafayette as a lieutenant general in 1791. Portrait by Joseph-Désiré Court

Born Marie-Joseph Paul Yves Roch Gilbert du Motier de Lafayette on September 7, 1757, to an aristocratic French family, he was to become famous in the United States for his service to the cause of the American Revolution.

He was from a wealthy landowning family from the south of France. His father, a colonel in the French army, was killed during the Seven Years War before Lafayette's second birthday.

At the age of twelve, he lost both his mother and grandfather to death, leaving him a very wealthy orphan. He joined the army at the age of fourteen, and at the age of sixteen, he married Marie Adrienne Francoise de Noailles from one of the wealthiest families in France and who was related to the king.

Before his eighteenth birthday, he had become acquainted and enamored with what he had heard from his friends in the nobility of the movement for freedom from Britain, then going on in the American Colonies. Determined to be a part of what he saw as an opportunity for excitement, and possibly glory, in this struggle, he made plans to travel to America, convincing some of his young friends to accompany him. His station in French aristocracy had allowed him to gain the promise of a commission as a major general in America.

Arriving at Charleston in the summer of 1777, he was presented to the Continental Congress, where he offered his service as a volunteer without pay. Impressed by the young Frenchman's patriotic zeal, he was offered and accepted the commission as major general he had been promised before he sailed from France.

During that same summer, it was his good fortune to meet George Washington, who took an immediate liking to the young marquis. From that meeting, a friendship developed that was to last the remainder of Washington's life.

Lafayette was wounded at the Battle of Brandywine four days after his twentieth birthday and, after recovering, wintered with Washington at Valley Forge. When sent by Washington to glean what information he could on the British in Philadelphia, he led an American force at the Battle of Barren Hill.

He later participated in the battle of Monmouth, and following that battle, he returned home to use his influence to bring France into the war on the side of the Americans. He worked tirelessly to secure French assistance both financially and militarily during almost a year and one-half in France. Eventually successful, in early 1780, he returned to America and the American Army where he again distinguished himself during the remainder of the war.

After the war, he returned home where he served in various capacities in French government and politics during the remainder of his life.

He twice returned to triumphant tours of the United States where he was honored with citizenship.

Lafayette died on May 20, 1834, and is buried in Paris under soil from Bunker Hill.

George Washington

George Washington was born on February 22, 1732, in Westmoreland County, Virginia. His parents were Augustine Washington and his second wife, Mary Ball Washington.

During his teens, he received training as a surveyor and through his older brother Lawrence, who had married Anne Fairfax, developed a friendship with that family. Through his connection to the Fairfax family, he was able to become familiar with much of Virginia and the western frontier.

His military career began in 1754 at the age of twenty-two, when he was commissioned as a lieutenant colonel of the Virginia Militia by the royal governor of the colony. He served in this capacity in campaigns on the frontier and later with the British during the French and Indian War. In 1758, he resigned his commission and settled into the life of a planter and a politician at his beloved Mount Vernon, which he had inherited upon the death of his brother Lawrence and the subsequent remarriage of Lawrence's widow.

In January 1759, Washington married Martha Dandridge Custis, a wealthy widow, thus furthering his position in Virginia society and politics. Very successful as a farmer, he was able to avoid the massive debt many Virginia tobacco farmers experienced by diversifying the cash crops grown at Mount Vernon.

During his planter years prior to the Revolution, he concentrated his efforts on improving Mount Vernon and his business interests. He was however, a vocal opponent of the 1765 Stamp Act, the Townshend Acts, and he regarded the passage of the

Intolerable Acts in 1774 as "an Invasion of our Rights and Privileges." That year, he chaired a meeting of Virginia delegates at which the convening of a Continental Congress was proposed. Later the same year, he was selected as a delegate to the First Continental Congress by the First Virginia Convention.

During the Second Continental Congress, he attended in military uniform and was nominated by John Adams of Massachusetts to be commander in chief of the newly created Continental Army. Approved by a vote of the Congress, Washington assumed command of the Continental Army in the field at Cambridge, Massachusetts, in July 1775, during the ongoing siege of Boston.

During the next eight years, he led the often beleaguered Continental Army through periods of both elation and despair, holding the colonies together often by only the strength of his own personal bravery, resolve, and strength of character. He would inflict the final blow to the British, with the help of the French, at the Virginia port of Yorktown in October 17, 1781, which ended all major fighting in America.

After the signing of the Treaty of Paris formally ended the war in 1783, he rejected the wish of many that he be honored as the sovereign of the newly established nation. Instead, he resigned his commission as commander in chief, bade farewell to the remaining officers and troops, and retired once again to the life of a gentleman farmer.

In 1787, he was persuaded to attend the Constitutional Convention in Philadelphia and was unanimously elected president of that Convention. With him in mind, delegates to the Convention designed the office of president, and with his recommendation, the new Constitution was ratified by all thirteen states. Two years later, in 1789 and again in 1792, the Electoral

College elected Washington president by a unanimous vote, the only president to receive 100 percent of the electoral votes.

After retiring from the presidency, Washington returned to Mount Vernon and re-devoted himself to his first love, which had always been farming.

On December 12, 1799, in miserably inclement weather, he spent the day on horseback, inspecting his farms, as was his custom. Upon returning home, he sat down to his evening supper without removing his wet clothes. The next morning, he awoke with respiratory symptoms which turned into acute laryngitis and pneumonia. The following day, on the evening of December 14, 1799, Washington died at his beloved Mount Vernon. He was only sixty-seven years old. A funeral was held on December 18, 1799, at Mount Vernon, and he was interred in a tomb on his beloved estate.

George Washington was mourned throughout the world, and Representative Henry Lee, a Revolutionary War comrade and father of the Civil War general Robert E. Lee, famously eulogized Washington as follows:

> First in war, first in peace, and first in the hearts of his countrymen, he was second to none in humble and enduring scenes of private life. Pious, just, humane, temperate, and sincere; uniform, dignified, and commanding; his example was as edifying to all around him as were the effects of that example lasting…Correct throughout, vice shuddered in his presence and virtue always felt his fostering hand. The purity of his private character gave effulgence to his public virtues…Such was the man for whom our nation mourns.

PROLOGUE

January 24, 1837

THE OLD MAN slumped back in his chair, as he came to the end of his story, exhausted from the effort to recall and relate to the court officer his experiences of some sixty years past, during the American Revolution. He had traveled to the courthouse in Burke County, North Carolina, from his home in nearby Lincoln County, where he had lived for over fifty years. The trip had been made in an attempt to secure the benefits of the Congressional service pension act of June 7, 1832. This last and most liberal act, of those benefitting Revolutionary War veterans, provided full pay to all those who had served at least two years in the military service of the United States during the Revolution. His service more than qualified him for the pension and, at this time of his life, would have been of great benefit to him and his wife.

He had come far from his humble beginnings in the Rhine River Valley of Germany. His journey had included an ocean voyage fraught with danger, eighteen months in indentured servitude and eight years in the armies of his adopted country. His advancing age prevented him from doing manual work and his deafness prevented him from continuing his previous vocation as a school teacher. Now nearing eighty years of age and nearly deaf, he had suffered financial setbacks during the last few years, which had left him with little to help him provide for himself and his wife. Much of the property he once owned had been lost through deals with unscrupulous individuals, who had taken advantage of his lack of understanding of the law and had left him in a situation becoming increasingly more difficult as the days passed.

Mr. Abner Payne, the court officer, taking the elderly man's statement, had struggled through the several hours of his declaration before he was satisfied that he had understood and had transcribed everything which had been related to him. The softness of the old man's voice and the names and places of which he spoke, many unknown to him, required that the he ask many questions. Although necessary, his questions and the old man's hearing loss extended the length of their interview and left both men near exhaustion at its completion.

The interview over, Payne could only marvel at the account which had just been related to him. It seemed to him a story which would have been impossible to have fabricated or made up. No one, he thought to himself, could have imagined such a tale, without having lived it and he felt certain the account would provide the assistance the old soldier so badly needed. In this assumption, he would be proven wrong, for despite the detailed declaration and the additional correspondence over the next eleven years, no pension would be allowed the aging man. It seemed that the his failure to keep his discharge papers, over the fifty-plus years since his service, and the lack of supporting muster rolls of the units in which he served would provide the pension board all they required to disallow the desperate request.

1

THE VOYAGE

ISAAC LEVAN ARRIVED with his companions at the Port of Rotterdam sometime in the late spring of 1773. Here they were plied with food and drink by those who earned their living providing the hopeless with hope and ship's captains with crew and passengers. Their fate, unknown to them, would be as servants, sold into indenture, for their passage to the Colonies. After their confidence was gained, Levan and his companions were soon taken on board the ship *Sally* captained by John Osmond, who was an experienced ship's captain, having previously delivered at least five other similar cargoes. This was not his largest cargo, but the passenger list was still quite substantial, at between two hundred and two hundred and fifty people. The ratio of male to female was approximately two males for each female, with almost all being "redemptioners." The term "redemptioners" was given to those individuals unable to pay their passage and consequently were required, at the end of their long voyage, to become indentured servants. The ship's agent or captain was responsible for collecting payment for their passage from the individual to whom they became indentured.

After all preliminary preparations were complete and provisions laid in the hold, the passengers, who were being kept in lodging near the docks, were taken on board and the *Sally* lifted anchor. The ship sailed down the Meuve and into the North

Sea, turning southward toward the channel separating France and England.

After a few days at sea, stopping briefly at Dover, the ship reached the city of Portsmouth. The day after arriving, June 4, 1773, those aboard were treated to a great celebration by the people of the city and to an elaborate military display from the many ships of the line, anchored in the port. The celebration proclaimed the birthday of his majesty King George III. While anchored at Portsmouth, where she cleared customs, the *Sally* took on final provisions of fresh meat and beer, sails were repaired, and all preparations were made to ready the ship for its journey across the ocean to America. When all was in readiness, she lifted anchor and set sail for Philadelphia and a new life for over two hundred new American citizens.

The first days of the journey passed uneventfully while Levan and his companions began to settle into the monotonous routine of an eighteenth century voyage between the old world and the new. This monotony would soon become a thing to be cherished, as after only a few days at sea, the *Sally* was greeted by a menacing wind, which blew the ship off course. It violently rocked to and fro, creating sickness among the passengers and much of the crew, including the captain himself. The storm lasted the better part of two days and, almost as quickly as it came, was gone. Adding to the misery of those who had been so violently ill, higher than normal winds remained until finally they subsided and tranquility return to the deep blue-green waters. Many, who had been sick for days, could only now begin to eat once again, with any hope of keeping down what they ate. The rejoicing that accompanied the tempest's end was to be interrupted by a second outburst more violent than the first. The first had weakened parts of the ship and what it had started, the new one finished, only adding to the almost constant maintenance needed on a sailing ship of the day. This new storm sent waves crashing over the deck, tearing away the railing and ship's privacy chambers which were attached. There had been little room for modesty before, but now, all pretense of privacy was removed.

Levan's shipmate, Johann Carl Buettner, speaks to these conditions in his memoirs which are quoted in his own words:

> The loss of these (the privacy chambers) was hard on all of us; especially on the women. For they, while performing the duties of nature, had to forego all sense of shame. Each one, when one wished to relieve oneself, must hold to the ships rope with one hand, while with the other, hold ones clothes over ones head and let oneself be splashed by the brine whenever the waves ran high enough. Mentioning this indecency forced upon us by necessity, I wish to speak about a far more serious and deplorable custom which was permitted on this transportation boat. Men and women did not sleep in separate cabins; the sixty girls were distributed among the three hundred men in their quarters. It can be easily understood how wide, under these circumstances, the doors of immorality were opened. I see tears in the eyes of the angel of innocence and he covers his face. Perhaps such reprehensible practices are no longer in force on transport ships, and should they be, I wish that the philanthropic statesman of Holland, the noble-minded Baron of Gagern, might succeed in ending them.
>
> I would advise unmarried women who have not the means to take quarters in the Captain's cabin, not even to enter a ship. Their innocence is much more in danger

than on land. Some one may bring up the question: Why did the captain permit persons of different sexes to spend the night together on his ship? Oh! If I did not have to answer that a pernicious, unpardonable love of money, the root of all evil, was at the bottom of this! Of course, the ship's captain could expect to receive for a woman who was with child a greater amount of money upon landing in America. Many of the girls on board died a frightful death before the ship landed. Once they contracted the loathsome disease, by some called the "gallant" one (editor's note: likely gonorrhea or syphilis), they usually met their cruel end. This will surprise no one who knows the character of this terrible disease and the conditions necessary for its cure. The treatment of this disease calls specifically for fresh nourishing food, pure air and good nursing. All of these are lacking on board a ship. The women worst infected were taken into a separate cabin under the capstan, where they died in unutterable misery. No one came near this spot unless obliged to, because of the horrible odor that prevailed there. The deceased were sewed up in a piece of sail cloth, a bag filled with sand was tied to the feet, and they were buried in the waves of the sea. Usually the bodies thrown into the water were immediately claimed as prey by the big fish. The captain found that if a number of these fish were swimming near the ship in the morning, he might conclude that corpses had been thrown overboard in the night.

Whitehead's description of the ship's accommodations differ somewhat from that of Buettner but does allude to the immorality, which in time added to the disease aboard, which afflicted many of the young and foolish, among the passengers.

He records that the ship was divided into thirty-six apartments, which he calls Coigs, each containing six or eight men, who were called messmates. The messmates took turns collecting and cooking the day's rations. Each man was required to wash his own clothes, unless as Whitehead put it, "such had in possession, a female favorite" to do it for him. He does not mention how the women's accommodations differed, if so, from those of the men.

Days at sea turned into weeks, and as the time passed, the misery of the ship's passengers worsened. The stench from the sheer number of people packed so tightly together was almost unbearable. Many suffered with various types of illnesses: seasickness, fevers, dysentery, rash, and other forms of disease, caused by the extremely poor diet. Whitehead's description of the symptoms, which many exhibited, indicates that they likely suffered from an outbreak of typhus. The suffering from the many various afflictions struck all equally, both passengers and crew. At times, so few of the crew were able to perform their duties that it became necessary that others from the ship's number be enlisted to assist with the requirements of sailors.

The death rate was extraordinarily high, estimated from the accounts of Buettner and Whitehead at 25 percent of those on board, both passenger and crew. This would indicate a death toll between sixty and seventy human beings.

Many cried out in their despair and wished they could somehow be miraculously returned to Germany and the life they had previously found so undesirable.

Buettner's narrative continues:

> After some time, I had a very violent fever that, as my companions told me, brought me very near death. I suffered utter delirium, and the surgeon was obliged to let

blood from both my arms of which I knew nothing. Of this attack I remember naught save the torture like the suffering of the damned that I saw constantly in my dreams. After I had recovered my mental balance, I often prayed with all my soul for the forgiveness of my trespasses and sins. I was quite aware that I had not respected the commands of our holy God. By the help of God I soon recovered fully. Our progress was very slow as we had most of the time winds from the wrong direction. Since our departure from the English coast, fifteen weeks had passed, while we were on the high seas and without sight of any land.

For the rest of the journey, the inhabitants of the *Sally* would struggle with the difficulties visited upon them by the various discomforts and diseases, which routinely plagued the ship. They would then be presented with only two other situations of note. The first was the appearance of what the captain at first suspected to be a pirate ship. This vessel gave chase, prompting the captain to order all capable on deck, to present at least a pretense of strength. There were among the cabin passengers, those who had paid for their passage and those that had brought rifles which were intended to be sold or bartered in America. These were displayed so that the pirates might be convinced that the *Sally* would be a difficult prey. This brief but exciting departure from the otherwise routine of a day at sea ended as quickly as it had begun when the menacing vessel reversed its course and soon disappeared on the horizon.

The second situation occurred as the *Sally* neared the end of her voyage. The captain, upon consulting his instruments, promised America would be sited the next day. (Although Buettner mentions fifteen weeks having passed, the length of the voyage is uncertain, as Whitehead's narrative records that they arrived at Portsmouth on the third day of June. Their arrival in Philadelphia is recorded by the date the passengers took the Oath of Allegiance as before August 13, a span of only eleven weeks). The captain's prediction was fulfilled, and the next day, all rejoiced at the first sighting of America. But to the dismay of all on board, the joy of sighting land for the first time in over two months would be short-lived. Before any preparation could be made for the ship to be guided passed the dangerous shoals and into Delaware Bay, a storm rose up once again, punishing the ship with the forces of nature.

Once again, Buettner describes what transpired:

> It was a windless, murky August day. The sea shone like a great clear mirror framed in the coast of America; hardly a breath of air rippled the water's surface but a countless multitude of fishes could be seen playing around the boat. Even the monsters of the deep raised their huge awkward bodies close to the surface with an undulating motion, and then sank again to the black depths where they belonged, and then the captain said to us: 'Children, pray, we are going to have a storm.' Soon we heard a distant rumbling; the sun began to darken; everything on the boat was in the greatest commotion in which many human voices mingled; with all possible speed the seamen furled the sails and bound them fast. The American pilots turned and hurried with their little boats coast ward. The hatches were closed and over them were nailed pieces of strong canvas soaked in tar. Ever stronger and more terrifying became the roaring of the hurricane. Like black, forbidding chains of mountains we saw the waves piled up by the storm bearing down upon us. The light-

ning tore through the frightfully black heavens and the thunder roared. Suddenly the ship flew like a ball, now among the clouds, and now as swift as an arrow, into the trough of the sea. All around powerful bolts of lightning fell into a fearfully raging sea, and the thunder exploded with terrific report. In inexpressible rage the waves beat against the ship, or coming from opposite directions collided with each other above the decks.

Every minute was as if we were suffering the most terrific bombardment. Every one was praying, and even the nefarious and the God-forsaken, of which there were plenty on board the ship, folded their hands as the Lord of the worlds spoke to them through the heart- crushing voice of the elements.

As the sun on the following day scattered his rays over a quiet sea, I, with many others, in prayer and song, thanked the Lord who helps, and even in the mercy of His judgment, saves from death. Oh, how unworthy of His grace were the most of us on board that ship! Our eyes could no longer see the coast of America, so longed for and so joyfully hailed. The drinking water became scarce, and for this reason we did not receive more than half a measure of water daily. Besides, this had a very unpleasant smell and tasted like ink. Notwithstanding, they fed us day after day with salted meat that increased our thirst. We received cheese on certain days. In need of more fluid, I gladly exchanged as did many others, my portion of cheese for half a measure of water.

To prevent myself from drinking more water than absolutely necessary to quench the thirst from which I constantly suffered, I stuck a quill through the cork of the water bottle and drew in the fluid slowly. Not only did this portion of water that we received not suffice to quench our thirst, but it was also needed to soften the ship's biscuit, to cook the peas, the oatmeal, and the meat. The bread that we received was so hard that an axe was required to break it, and it looked green and yellow inside. The peas were only half cooked and were very difficult to digest. We liked best the oat meal rations. It can easily be seen why we desired even more than ever to reach dry land, and why we were more than happy when we sighted it for the second time, after a lapse of three long weeks. Again the pilots that we had seen once before came toward us in their little boats, and this time guided us successfully into the great arm of the sea leading to Philadelphia, called Delaware Bay, which is eighty miles long and three miles wide. But yet eight days passed before we reached Philadelphia, because the ship could proceed only very slowly on account of the current of the Delaware. We anchored amid stream in the river and took delight in gazing at the great beautiful city of Philadelphia.

2

ARRIVAL

THE *SALLY* ARRIVED within sight of America's largest city, the third week of August 1773. The next day, doctors were brought on board to ensure that the passengers and crew carried no plague or epidemic, which could be introduced into the population of Philadelphia. Finding nothing of concern, the doctors returned to the city, and the next day, all male passengers aged sixteen and over, were transported ashore, where they swore allegiance to the Church of England and his majesty King George III.

The weary immigrants soon faced their first disappointment upon their arrival in America. Having endured weeks without good water or fresh food, Isaac Levan and the other redemptioners on board, eagerly anticipated the change of diet they expected the arrival to bring. In this, they would initially be frustrated. To their dismay, the usual provisions continued except for water, which was available at their pleasure and some fresh mutton, which replaced the salted beef provided during the passage. They would find this to be the case until they were "redeemed" by someone who would pay for their passage or for those who had the money to purchase fresh produce from the vendors who came aboard. Some chose to sell or exchange what personal possessions they could part with to improve their fare. At this effort, they often fell victim to those seeking to take advantage of their naivety. Sadly, these swindlers would often be their own countrymen who had preceded them in immigration and looked to take their possessions for a fraction of their real worth. The second disappointment for many would be the wait they would have to endure before someone would agree to an arrangement, which would settle their debt. A debt, which in most cases, far exceeded what the new citizens of America had expected. Most had been quoted a cost of passage by the captain before leaving Rotterdam. But they found these debts had been significantly increased by items for which they were indebted that they had not suspected. None had factored into their debt, the bounty which had been paid to the "soul vendors," who delivered them to their point of departure and who had provided them with food, drink, and lodging until they could be delivered to a ship. Other unexpected additions to their debt were the cost of items issued while on board ship, which were not included among the "common provisions" issued as part of their passage. These included rum, tea, sugar and other items issued unequally, to individuals, as they requested them, but whose cost was shared equally by all. The *Sally's* passengers were also charged equally with the debts of those who had perished at sea. This was against the prevailing law of the time which required these debts to be paid by family members. However, because many of the passengers had no family on board or no family in either their new homeland or their old, to pay these debts, the law was quickly circumvented to prevent these debts from being absorbed by the captain or the ship agents and owners.

A day after the *Sally's* arrival, those seeking to find for themselves suitable servants, whose passage they would pay in return for an agreed upon period of service, began to come aboard ship to make their selection. The cost of passage was very similar for all; therefore, the negotiations dealt primarily with the length of the indenture. The length of service for those on the *Sally* ranged primarily between four and seven years, with those persons considered most desirable receiving the lesser period.

Levan, being slight of build and considerably weakened from the three months at sea, presented a less than attractive picture to those seeking strong young men for the farm work many of them needed. Because of this, Levan would continue to languish another three weeks before being liberated from the ship.

Finally during the middle of the second week of September, Captain Osmond, in the company of a man dressed more in the manner of a merchant than that of a farmer, approached Levan. As they came closer, the captain pointed at Levan and spoke to the man who accompanied him.

"Mr. Boyes, here is a young man who may well be more suited to your trade. He has been passed over by those looking for farm laborers, but I judge him to be healthy and strong for his size."

Levan was told to stand and turn so that he could be viewed from all sides. As he stood silently without being addressed by either of the men, he was poked and prodded and examined like a young calf at auction.

After his examination, the men stepped away and began a conversation, presumably discussing what was to be paid to the captain to release Levan from the debt owed for his passage. Eventually, an agreement was reached and the man shook the captain's hand and the two men again approached him and he was informed his debt of twenty-seven pounds and thirteen shillings would be paid and he would be released to the man whose name was William Boyes. It would later be determined that Levan be held in servitude for a period of seven years to repay the debt purchased by Mr. Boyes. Once their bargain had been struck, Levan and his new master left the ship, and after a short journey, they soon arrived at what would become Levan's new home.

Levan was quickly introduced to the rest of the household and mercifully fed the first decent meal he had consumed since leaving Amsterdam.

Life as a servant was often hard, but his circumstances were more favorable than many of those arriving in the pre-revolution colonies. He found it much better than his life had been in his native Germany. There, on his own, he had been forced to struggle for survival. An opportunity for life in the new world, even if it meant spending seven years indentured, seemed to him, at least initially, a tolerable bargain. As excessive as it later began to feel, he hoped that his time as a servant would help him learn a trade which he could use to make a life for himself, when his period of indenture was complete.

His master, a Quaker, was the proprietor of a bakery, and upon his arrival, Levan was quickly put to work as an apprentice baker. Due to his master's religious convictions, he was treated with kindness and compassion and was allowed to sleep in a back room of the bakery and eat his meals with the family. This was in stark contrast to many of those indentured, whose circumstances were much different and more difficult than his. With a warm place to sleep, plenty to eat, and a kind family to live among, he counted himself blessed, despite the long hours of hard work in the bakery. He felt his treatment most fair because the Boyes family worked the long hours as well. He developed, at least on a limited basis, a bond with the children, with whom he was able to enjoy the pastimes of youth when the opportunity presented itself.

These circumstances, although comfortable, still did not quiet the stirrings in his adventurous nature, which had led him to make the arduous crossing of the Atlantic, to this new land. His first year in his newly adopted country was spent almost exclusively at the will of his master and allowed for little time of his own. He made only a few friends, mostly from among those like himself, who had lacked the cost of passage and now found themselves trapped in a life of servitude, which would consume much of their youth and limit their futures in this land of seemingly endless opportunity. They all had heard stories of the opening frontier where land was available for those willing to brave the hostility of the untamed wilderness. Many of the more adventurous ones yearned to be able to strike out and make a life of their own. There were, however, strong chains holding them in place until they were free of their indentures and were able to save enough to purchase what would be needed to make such a bold move.

There were strong deterrents to leaving a life of certainty for a life of uncertainty. Stiff penalties faced those who took flight and were caught and returned. Along with the anxiety of beginning a new life with only the clothes on their back, they faced the uncertainty of where to go with no means of transportation to carry them to whatever destination they chose.

When able to speak to each other beyond the ears of their masters or the ears of those who might bring such talk to their master's attention, some servants plotted their escape, and some, despite the dangers involved, managed to gain their freedom at least temporarily. Levan, for whatever reason was able to avoid the temptation to run away, and soon was presented with an opportunity, not carrying with it the brand of "runaway," but including its own element of uncertainty.

1774 was a year of remarkable change in the American Colonies. In December of 1773, only four months after his arrival in America, an event would take place in the city of Boston,

Massachusetts, which would in part, set in motion a chain of events which would alter his life forever. This event, commonly referred to as the "Boston Tea Party,"[1] was an outward display of anger, resentment, and disobedience to the English crown and would trigger other events both in the Colonies and by the English Parliament.

By the fall of 1774, after a year in Pennsylvania, Levan had begun to pick up the English language and although still limited in his ability to read the city's papers, his verbal comprehension was becoming quite good. The air of revolution was widespread in the city of Philadelphia. Everywhere he went, he heard the heated discussions, both for and against, separation from England.

---

[1] From Wikipedia, the free encyclopedia

The Boston Tea Party was a direct action by colonists in Boston, a town in the British colony of Massachusetts, against the British government. On December 16, 1773, after officials in Boston refused to return three shiploads of taxed tea to Britain, a group of colonists boarded the ships and destroyed the tea by throwing it into Boston Harbor. The Tea Party was the culmination of a resistance movement throughout British America against the Tea Act, which had been passed by the British Parliament in 1773. Colonists objected to the Tea Act for a variety of reasons, especially because they believed that it violated their right to be taxed only by their own elected representatives. Protesters had successfully prevented the unloading of taxed tea in three other colonies, but in Boston, embattled Royal Governor Thomas Hutchinson refused to allow the tea to be returned to Britain. He apparently did not expect that the protestors would choose to destroy the tea rather than concede the authority of a legislature in which they were not directly represented.

It was the most common topic on the street and even at church services, which he was allowed to attend because of his master's religious conviction. Although the Boyes family was Quaker, Levan was allowed to attend services of his choice. He sometimes attended the Lutheran Church, with which he had become familiar in Germany. In addition to overheard conversations, he was also able to read those same conflicting sentiments in past issues of the German language newspapers, which he was frequently given by members of the German community he came in contact with, while delivering goods to the homes of the bakery's customers.

Much of the talk centered on what were being called by many, the "Intolerable Acts,"[2] (Exhibit II) forced by the English Parliament, on Boston, the Massachusetts Bay Colony, and in the two most recent acts, all of the remaining colonies.

These acts, which had been passed during the first six months of 1774, partly in retaliation for the Boston Tea Party, had led to a congress of delegates, from all the colonies except Georgia.

Those chosen as delegates from Georgia were blocked from attending by Georgia's royal governor whose allegiance was to the Crown.

The congress[3] (Exhibit III) held in September of 1774 in Levan's own Philadelphia, had been deemed necessary, even

---

[2] From Wikipedia, the free encyclopedia

The Intolerable Acts or the Coercive Acts are names used to describe a series of laws passed by the British Parliament in 1774 relating to Britain's colonies in North America. The acts sparked outrage and resistance in the Thirteen Colonies and were important developments in the growth of the American Revolution.

[3] The First Continental Congress was a convention of delegates from twelve of the thirteen North American colonies that met

though the first three acts had little if any effect on any of the colonies, except for Massachusetts. They did serve, however, to engender the sympathies of the remaining twelve for their sister colony. What could be done to one, some believed, could be done to all. The Quartering Act and the Quebec Act were a different story, as they affected all thirteen Colonies, and the Quebec Act, affecting the New England Colonies in particular. It raised concern with regard to the spread of the influence of the French Catholics and the potential of a state church in Quebec. It was especially troublesome to the German Christians of several sects, including Quakers, Lutherans and Huguenots, who made up a significant part of the population of Pennsylvania, and Philadelphia, its largest city in particular.

The delegates to the Congress had addressed these acts with the following objectives: to compose a statement of colonial rights to identify the British Parliament's violation of those rights, and to develop a plan, convincing Parliament to restore those rights. The results of the Congress mattered little as King George had apparently already come to a decision on his actions in the Colonies. On September 11, 1774, he wrote in his diary: "The die is now cast. The colonies must either submit or triumph. I do not wish to come to severer measures, but we must not retreat."

Two months later on November 18, he wrote: "Blows must decide whether they are to be subject to this country or independent."

The die was indeed cast, and Isaac Levan would soon be swept up in the monumental events to come. It is unlikely that

---

on September 5, 1774, at Carpenters' Hall in Philadelphia, Pennsylvania.

he could envision in his wildest imagination what would lie before him in the next eight years.

In January 1775, Massachusetts governor, Thomas Gage was ordered to move against the Massachusetts rebels and to arrest the leaders of the Continental Congress. His orders included using force of arms if it was required.

Before these orders arrived in Boston, the Massachusetts Provisional Congress, which had been formed in October of the previous year, met on February 1 in Cambridge. The meeting led to the beginning of defensive preparations for a state of war and the organization and equipping of a militia, ready for an anticipated but unwanted war. These two incidents, though unrelated due to the time required for news to be passed by ship between Great Britain and the Colonies, significantly impacted the mood of the colonist. They especially affected those in port cities where the news would first arrive. People throughout the Colonies would become more outraged, as the news of these events and those, which would quickly follow, unfolded. Colonial militias, if not already in existence, would soon be authorized and raised in all the Colonies, including Pennsylvania. Those in Pennsylvania would often be raised, despite the objections by some of the leading Quakers in the Colony, against any military action against the British.

One of the early units raised in Philadelphia was a battalion of men of German ancestry, to which Levan would soon be drawn. The Dutch Battalion, as Levan refers to it in his declaration, began forming during the winter months of early 1775. Levan was intrigued with the possibilities that joining this new military unit might offer him. There were rumors that those enlisting would receive a monthly payment and upon completion of three years' service would receive one hundred and sixty acres of land. The prospect of ending his remaining years of servitude, the opportunity for land of his own and the adventure and excitement offered by military service soon became an enticement he could not resist, and on March 3, 1775, Isaac Levan became a soldier.

3

1775—OFF TO WAR

BY THE BEGINNING of 1775, the British government had become increasingly concerned about the growing number of militia units being raised in the Colonies, especially in Massachusetts which seemed to the Crown to be at the heart of the movement of resistance to British policies in the Colonies. In order to suppress any potential armed resistance, General Thomas Gage, the military governor of Massachusetts and commander in chief of the roughly three thousand British military forces in Boston, was ordered to confiscate suspected caches of weapons and supplies, especially those belonging to members of the militia and to imprison the leaders of the perceived rebellion.

In late April, news of this British plan and the subsequent battles between the British regulars and Massachusetts militia, at Lexington and Concord (Exhibit IV) reached other areas of the Colonies, enflaming further an already tenuous situation throughout those previously unaffected by direct confrontation. At the same time, militia units in these areas had begun to form, including the city of Philadelphia, where Levan's Dutch Battalion would be formed. Some colonial leaders had envisioned a plan to gain control of the upper Hudson River Valley by capturing the British forts near Lake George, which controlled the Hudson Valley and the route to Canada. They hoped by doing so they could mount an invasion of Canada and draw Canadians into the conflict as allies to the American cause. Many of those who favored a break from Britain believed that many in Canada would rally to the cause of the American Colonies and join them in their quest for Independence. If they could convince the Canadians to support a break from England, there would be less concern of a threat from the north.

Once the forts along Lake George had been captured and their military stores secured, the plan called for military movement on Montreal and Quebec in hopes that the inhabitants of those cities would rally to the colonial cause. One of the units dispatched to capture the Lake George forts was the Dutch Battalion, which included a newly formed company of which the young German was now a member. The company had begun enlisting men during the winter and, in short order, had begun training exercises to ensure it would be ready at the initiation of any hostilities. It is uncertain when Levan's unit marched out of Philadelphia, as Levan's pension declaration only mentions that their march began on the fifth, giving no month. It is likely that they left either the fifth of March or of April as their destination proved to be the forts along Lake George in upstate New York, a distance of almost 300 miles. This distance alone and the fact that they arrived by the first week of May is a clear indication that they did not leave Philadelphia after hearing of the battles at Bunker Hill and Lexington. Levan's company marched northeast along what was known as the King's Highway thru New Jersey to New York City, where they turned north on the Albany Post Road, along the Hudson River Valley to Fort Edward. The fort, originally built at the outbreak of hostilities between the French and English in the early 1750s, was named for Edward, the Duke of York, and the younger brother of King George III. It was constructed and garrisoned by the English to prevent French incursion into the Hudson Valley. Following the French and Indian War, Fort Edward was evacuated and the stores and cannons moved to other fortifications in the area including the fort at Crown Point. Fort Edward was left to be reclaimed by its natural surroundings. Although in ruins, it was strategically positioned along what has been called the Great Military Warpath and the Hudson River. Only empty barracks remained of the fort, but they would serve as shelter for troops moving through the area during the American Revolution, including Levan's Company.

The march to Fort Edward presented Levan and most of his comrades with their first exposure to the American frontier. Their march began as winter was loosening its grip on Pennsylvania and New York and ended in the early days of spring. This transition from winter to spring presented a diversity of weather which would subject them in the early part of the march, to frigid nights, blustery snowy days, and in the last weeks, the warmth of the spring sun and with it, frequent gentle spring rains. Their march took them through the farm lands of Pennsylvania and New Jersey before reaching the dense forest along the Hudson River Valley. Daily, the landscape changed, as farmers began to prepare their fields for the crops on which their lives depended. The trees changed from bleak stick figures to miracles of blooms and newly budding leaves to complement the numerous varieties of wildflowers which grew along the route. Throughout, there was one constant that seemed always to be with the marching men and that was the mud that accompanies winter's thaw and early spring rains adding to what was already a laborious effort. If these hardships were not enough, there was also the hunger from lack of supplies. The plentiful game found in the surrounding fields and forest helped alleviate the hunger but could not provide all the nutritional needs of active men.

Despite the hardships endured, the Dutch Battalion reached Fort Edward the first week in May and remained there only a few days before participating in the capture of the forts around Lake George.

The first fort to fall to the Americans was Ticonderoga on May 10, 1775. At the same time, Levan and members of his Dutch Battalion were moving up the valley from Albany, a force of militia commanded by Ethan Allen was moving toward Lake George from the East. It would be Allen and his Green Mountain Boys, accompanied by Benedict Arnold and members of Levan's battalion, including Levan, who would seize Ticonderoga with relative ease.

In the following days, Fort George and Crown Point along with their artillery and stores would also fall to the Americans with little resistance from the British.

The captured cannons along with tons of shot would later be removed from the forts by General Henry Knox and would play a significant role in driving the British out of Boston Harbor. The stores and provisions captured would be of much more immediate importance, helping to alleviate the day to day struggle to feed the increasing number of men now involved in the push northward. The seizures would also provide them with powder and musket balls that would be needed in the soon to follow invasion of Canada.

Upon securing Crown Point, Arnold moved on the small town of Skenesboro capturing several flat-bottom boats and a schooner belonging to the man who had founded the town. Arnold immediately left on the schooner, which he renamed *Liberty* and outfitted with guns. Additional troops followed, with men rowing the flat-bottom boats, but they were soon outdistanced by Arnold, who had the advantage of sail. His objective was the fort and shipyards at St. Jean, at the upper end of Lake Chaplain. The garrison at the fort was surprised and quickly subdued and the stores captured along with a newly completed British sloop which Arnold renamed *The Enterprise* and later outfitted with twelve cannons. Receiving news that word had reached the British of the loss of the forts along Lake George and that British forces might be moving south from Montreal, Arnold returned to his ships and began the return trip to Skenesboro. On the trip back, they met Ethan Allen and the men in the flat-bottom boats, with whom they shared their captured provisions and held a brief celebration.

Allen, determined to push on to the fort which he was determine to hold, continued north while Arnold continued south. Upon arriving at the fort, Allen was warned, by a sympathetic citizen of Montreal, that a British force was approaching, forcing him to abandon the fort and return south to Ticonderoga.

The young Levan, while likely not involved in all of these actions, had been a participant in several and would soon be involved in dozens of operations to come, including the attack on Quebec, where he was to experience his first real combat.

Following the return to Crown Point and Ticonderoga, the men, who had experienced the euphoria of victory so soon in their military careers, would now have to settle into a period of inactivity while the Continental Congress decided what to do next.

Believing initially that abandoning the recently captured forts would be the best course of actions, the Congress was quickly persuaded by both Arnold and Allen, that not only was it important to keep the forts manned for protection from British incursion from Canada but that a better course of action would be to use the forts as a base of operations for an invasion of Canada.

The First Congress had sent letters to the French Canadians inviting them to join them for a second meeting to be held in May and the Second Congress, after meeting in May, sent a similar letter. Neither of the letters drew a response, and in late June, the Congress, after hearing of a British plan to bring the Iroquois into the conflict and to resupply and add additional troops at Fort St. Jean, authorized General Philip Schuyler to investigate. He was to determine if an invasion of Canada was the best course of actions for the newly created Continental Army under the leadership of Virginia's George Washington.

Arnold, who had played such a large role in the capture of the Hudson Valley forts, was passed over for command and General Schuyler given the responsibility for planning the movement on Canada. The plan called for the use of Ticonderoga as a base for a move up Lake Champlain to Fort St. Jean and then on to Montreal and Quebec. Arnold, not giving up on being a part of whatever was to take Gen. Philip Schuyler's place, traveled to Boston, met with Washington, and convinced the general to outfit him for a march directly northward through Maine, and then by river to Quebec, where he was to join Schuyler.

Ph: Schuyler

It would be several weeks before Schuyler would be ready to begin his movement north and, in the interim, much would be required to prepare the men for combat against British regulars who were arguably the finest soldiers in the world. It would be necessary to gather provisions to equip and sustain a force of possibly two thousand men. In addition, discipline would need to be instilled into the diverse units that made up the American forces so that they might operate as a unit and not as independent companies each one determining what to do and how to do it.

During these weeks of preparation, Levan found many reasons to question his decision to join the fight for independence. In addition to the daily drilling in preparation for the upcoming fight, there were the menial tasks shared mostly among the privates, which were all too similar to those expected of him as an indentured servant. Animals had to be cared for, water had to be carried from the nearest stream for both drinking and cooking, and the men had to be fed. Meals were usually prepared by members of a small group of messmates, who would draw rations and share the preparation, cooking and cleaning up, among the members of the group.

His experiences, while indentured, would serve him well during these periods of inactivity. The disciplined behavior he was used to enabled him to find something to busy himself with, thus avoiding the temptations that often befell the younger men, who all too often found themselves drawn into activities which would land them in trouble with their company sergeant.

When free time did come, it was usually accompanied by the boredom of life in a large camp with little to entertain them.

Some played active games, similar to those played among the Indians, while others played cards or games of chance.

But the worst part of the inactivity was the close proximity to so many strangers and the disease often spread among them.

For many, who had previously only had contact with a limited number of people and who lived in reasonably healthy conditions for the period, it was drastic change. It would be their first time sharing living conditions with a large group of people, each of them coming from a different lifestyle and having been exposed to the various diseases of the time.

Exposure to normal childhood diseases such as measles, malaria, dysentery, and worst of all, smallpox was common, and a normal day would find a significant percentage of the camp population unfit for duty of any kind. The constancy of disease would plague the soldiers throughout their wait for the movement on Quebec and also during the campaign itself.

Levan apparently made few lasting relationships during the first several months of his military service, as his declaration for pension makes no mention of the names of those who served with him during this period.

By the end of August, the army was provisioned and ready to move on Montreal.

On the last day of August, General Schuyler wrote General Washington, advising him that he had arrived at Ticonderoga:

> General Montgomery leaves Crown Point to-day, with twelve hundred men and four twelve-pounders. I follow him this evening, and have ordered the whole strength I can spare to join me at Isle aux Noix without delay. When they arrive there, which I hope will be in five days, I shall then be near two thousand strong. I am still of opinion that the Canadians and Indians will be friendly to us..... I will neither detain your Excellency, nor waste my time (which is precious) in giving you a detail of the many wants I labor under. I hope they will serve for an evening chat at some future day.

Almost three weeks to the day after his first letter, Schuyler wrote Washington, again from Ticonderoga, with a detailed report on the army's activities during that period. He had returned there due to illness and had turned over the invasion of Canada to General Richard Montgomery.

Rich.ᵈ Montgomery

General Richard Montgomery

His letter had little good news to report except for the capture of Isle-aux-Noix, an island on the Richelieu River south of Fort St. Jean, where they had received reinforcements. He noted the receipt of a letter from Washington, notifying him of Arnold's departure for Quebec. His letter was full of reports of illness among the troops stating that, "The number of sick is incredible, and I have very little assistance to afford them."

About the same time that Schuyler was writing his second letter, General Montgomery forces were finally successful in establishing a siege around Fort St. Jean, from which they were able to place mortar batteries to bombard the interior of the fort. The defenders were well-supplied with arms and munitions and resisted the siege, believing that it would be lifted by reinforcements under General Guy Carleton. Food and other types of supplies on the other hand were severely lacking.

Holding on despite the growing shortage of food, the defend-

General Sir Guy Carleton

Gov. Guy Carleton

ers resisted until they were finally forced to surrender on the third of November, after the fall of nearby Fort Chambly and the repulse of an attempt at relief by General Carleton.

The six-week siege had dramatically affected the American plans and delayed the movement on Montreal, which fell without a fight as Carleton fled to Quebec.

After taking control of Montreal, Montgomery headed for Quebec with only three hundred men, leaving the remainder to protect Montreal. The battle for Quebec would now have to take place during the Canadian winter instead of the fall, as had been originally planned, greatly dimming any prospects for a quick victory.

Arnold's forces arrived at Point Levis on November 8, which was situated on the St. Lawrence River, opposite Quebec. His march across country had left him with a poorly supplied force reduced by one-third, due to illness and the difficulty of the wilderness march and the onset of suffering from the effects of the rapidly approaching winter.

A few days after arriving in Quebec, he was able to cross the St. Lawrence and move his force to Point-Aux-Trembles, a short distance to the west of Quebec, where he was joined by Montgomery on December 3, 1775.

Moving and supplying an army was always a difficult task, but the rains and snows of winter turned the task from difficult to nearly impossible. Now after their arduous marches, Arnold and Montgomery were forced to lay siege to a fortified city, garrisoned by a fully entrenched force, equal or greater than their own and commanded by Carleton, a seasoned British officer. Carleton, too wise to leave his fortifications and take on the Americans in the open, was happy to remain inside and await an assault, which he had little doubt would come soon.

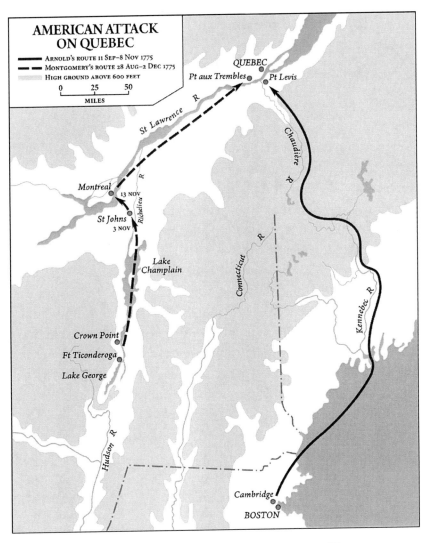

AMERICAN ATTACK ON QUEBEC

━━━ Arnold's route 11 Sep–8 Nov 1775
┅┅┅ Montgomery's route 28 Aug–2 Dec 1775
▒▒▒ High ground above 600 feet

0   25   50
MILES

QUEBEC

Pt aux Trembles

Pt Levis

St Lawrence R

Chaudière R

Montreal

13 NOV

Richelieu R

St Johns

3 NOV

Lake Champlain

Connecticut R

Kennebec R

Crown Point

Ft Ticonderoga

Lake George

Hudson R

Cambridge

BOSTON

Attack on Quebec US Army Center of Military History

Left with little choice, Arnold and Montgomery began their assault during the early morning hours of December 31 in a raging snowstorm, which they hoped would allow them to move their forces into position unnoticed. The plan called for Montgomery to attack the city along the river from the west, with his force, which included Levan's Dutch troops, while Arnold was to attack from the east. The two forces were to meet in the middle of the Lower Town and after joining forces march up the main route to Upper Town.

At approximately 4:00 a.m., on Montgomery's command, rockets were fired, signaling the attack to begin, and the two forces moved forward toward their objectives.

Montgomery, who was accompanied by his two aides, Captains John Macpherson and Jacob Cheesman, was at the head of the advancing force as it reached the western edge of Lower Town. As the three men moved forward for a better look at the defenses, they encountered a rough barricade. The barricade defenders fired on the three men, mortally wounding all three. Montgomery's second in command, Lieutenant Colonel Donald Campbell, immediately ordered a retreat and the men fell back out of range of fire. As Levan joined in the panicked retreat, he yelled out to no one in particular: "What has happened?"

"Our general has been shot" was the reply from an unknown voice.

"Is he dead?"

"I don't know, but I believe that he is." was the reply from the unknown voice.

Although not killed instantly, Montgomery was left on the field where he died and was later buried by the British. His death was an unfortunate blow to the Americans as Arnold's assault met with much more success.

At the signal of Montgomery's rockets, Arnold immediately launched his attack on the eastern edge of town where he encountered another heavily defended barricade. Arnold, leading the attack, was struck by a British musket ball, which shattered his left leg. His second in command, Captain Daniel Morgan, was nearby and had seen Arnold fall and rushed to his side.

"General," Morgan exclaimed, "how badly are you injured?"

"I think it not mortal," Arnold replied, "but I fear I am unable to continue."

"What are your orders, General? What would you have me do?"

"Push on, we have to support Montgomery," replied Arnold, who had no knowledge of Montgomery's fate.

After ensuring Arnold's removal from the field, Morgan, now in command, continued the assault, successfully overrunning the British barricades and reaching the center of Lower Town where he paused to await the arrival of Montgomery's men, which would never come. As the first light of dawn appeared behind him, Morgan's impatience finally overtook him and discarding the advice of his lieutenants, he pushed his men forward, but the advantage originally attained had been lost. The time lost in waiting for Montgomery had allowed Carleton to reposition his troops and to reinforce the barricades previously overcome. Morgan was now trapped. Eventually, almost all of Arnold's men were captured and the opportunity to seize control of Quebec was lost, ending the American dream of a Canadian alliance.

Levan's company and the remainder of the defeated Americans paused briefly at Wolfe's Cove to prevent the British from following their withdrawal, after successfully preventing an attempt by a few British boats from moving up river. As

Arnold recovered from his wound, which he would not allow to compel him to surrender his command, and with modest reinforcements from Montreal, he continued to besiege Quebec until March, when he was relieved and ordered to return to Montreal as post commander. His replacement, General David Wooster, continued the siege until he was replaced in late April by General John Thomas, who arrived from Boston, to find an increasingly deteriorating situation in Canada. The American Army was not only ravaged by an outbreak of smallpox but was now facing a superior British force reinforced by additional British Regiments along with German mercenaries. Additional troops under General John Burgoyne would arrive in May, swelling the British ranks to 13,000.

Faced with the overwhelming odds against him, Thomas quickly began to retreat from Quebec. During the retreat, he himself contracted smallpox and died in early June, replaced once again by a new American commander sent by Washington. The new commander, John Sullivan, would aggressively resist a complete withdrawal but would be compelled to do so after a disastrous defeat at Trois-Rivières, or Three Rivers.

Sullivan retreated south, along Lake Champlain, where he joined with Arnold at Ft. St. Jean, but the American army, although almost 8,000 strong was still no match for the pursuing British army. With their troops, exhausted, hungry, demoralized, and still suffering from smallpox, along with dysentery and malaria, the two commanders had no choice but to give up any hope of continuing the Canadian Campaign and retreat to Chambly and Crown Point.

4

1776—THE WAR EXPANDS

MEANWHILE, LEVAN'S COMPANY had been assigned to a new regiment authorized by Congress and designated the 2nd Canadian Regiment. It would become better known as Congress' Own, or Hazen's Regiment, for the man who would command it for the remainder of the war. Born in the colonies, Moses Hazen, who had previously served in the British Army during the French and Indian Wars, was living in Canada, near Fort St. Jean, when Montgomery attacked. Observing the capture of the fort at St. Jean in November, Hazen's allegiance was torn between the British, who offered him a commission, and the Americans. He was eventually drawn into the conflict and participated with the Americans in the siege of Quebec.

Following the defeat at Quebec, Hazen traveled to Philadelphia to report on the outcome of the battle at Quebec and, while there, received command of the new regiment, in partial payment of damages done to his property during the Canadian campaign.

In February, Hazen returned to Montreal, where he organized the regiment beginning with troops already in place, including Levan's Philadelphia Company. Additional recruits were to come from the area around Montreal and the St. Lawrence River Valley, with the maximum force to be 1,000, a number never reached. By April, with less than 300 men, Hazen's

Regiment was ordered south to guard the forts at Crown Point and Chambly. Once again, Levan's military experience would involve the day-to-day boredom of post duty.

By June, the retreating forces of Arnold and Sullivan had reached Chambly and Crown Point, with Arnold covering the withdrawal and burning or destroying anything thought to be of use to the British as he retreated. Defenses were set up to repel any advance by the British through the Hudson Valley, although Carleton did advance as far as Crown Point before being turned back by winter.

After arriving at Fort Chambly, in one of the sordid pages of the American Revolution, Arnold brought charges against General Hazen for dereliction of his duty while commanding Fort Chambly.

The charges brought by Arnold, stemmed from Hazen's failure to receive and to store supplies, commandeered by Arnold before leaving Montreal. It was also during this period that the Canadian Department was disbanded and Hazen's Regiment placed in the Northern Department under General Schuyler.

The supplies in question had been seized from local merchants, and receipts issued for the goods and identified so that the merchants could make claim for payment at a later date. These goods had been shipped to Chambly in early June, but Hazen, who owned property in the area and was acquainted with some of the merchants, refused to store the goods, believing that they had been improperly seized and that the merchants would never be properly repaid for their seizure.

Charges and countercharges flew until General Horatio Gates, now in command of all Northern forces, removed Arnold's arrest warrant and the matter was settled, with only the further sullying of both men's reputations. Once the differences between the two men were remedied, even if only temporarily, Hazen's regiment was ordered south to Albany and Levan was on the move once again. In November, the regiment was assigned to the Highlands Department before moving to winter quarters at Fishkill, New York, as described in Levan's declaration:

> "From there to work in New York and there joined Genl. Washington's army and the winter of 1776 was spent without having one settled place for winter quarters as the British was at Brunswick and Little Amboy and Elizabeth Town point so that we had to shift to guard them as we could."

The Highlands department was part of a force positioned to monitor the British during their occupation of New York City. Washington, with most of the American forces, moved south to lick its wounds from the disastrous campaign around New York, where Washington's army suffered successive defeats at Long Island, White Plains, and Fort Washington.

During this retreat, the American army was to suffer yet another indignation as General Charles Lee, who had recently returned from command of the Southern Department and placed in command of Washington's left wing, was to suffer capture by the British. The circumstances of the capture only added to the embarrassment. Lee, who had been ordered to follow the rest of the Continental Army on its retreat to Pennsylvania, dawdled and allowed the British to tighten the pursuit.

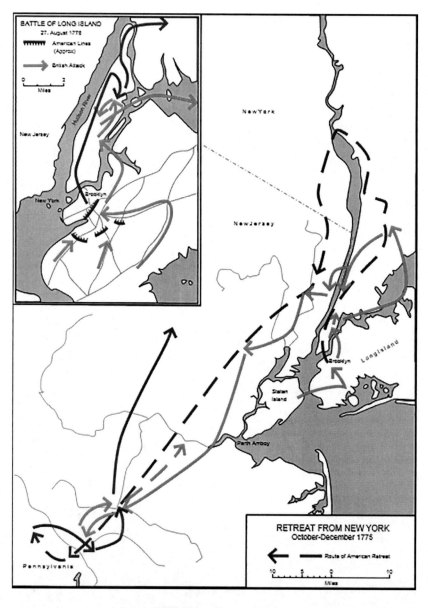

"NY-NJ-retreat-1776"
Licensed under Public Domain via Wikimedia Commons

Levan's makes mention of this event in his declaration:

"Genl. Lee commanded the 2nd Division that I was in and he left his Division at a creek and went to a tavern called Whites Tavern near Lord Sterling's buildings (referring to the home of Continental Genl. William Alexander, Lord Sterling) and was there taken prisoner by 5 or 6 British Dragoons."

Lee had made his camp a few miles south of Morristown, as he slowly made his way to join Gen. George Washington's force. Lee chose not to stay at the camp, but instead, in search of female companionship, he and a small entourage rode the three miles to White's Tavern, near Basking Ridge.

A cavalry detachment sent by British Commander Lord Cornwallis to determine the location of the American camp was informed of the location by a local Tory. After receiving that information, the British came upon and captured two American sentries, who told the British detachment that Lee and his guard were staying at the tavern. Uncertain of the truth of the information, Lt. Colonel Banastre Tarleton and two cavalrymen rode forward to verify the report. Tarleton was able to confirm Lee's location, and while his troops resumed their march, Lee remained at the tavern writing letters. Tarleton's men swept down on the tavern, overwhelming the American guard detachment and, after a short skirmish, captured Lee, still in his night shirt. After gathering up the wounded and the prisoners, the British headed back to their headquarters with Lee still in his nightshirt. A few American soldiers, who had avoided capture, escaped and returned to the American lines and reported Lee's capture. A search party sent out to look for

Lee was too late as the British forces had already reached their headquarters with Lee in tow.

While Hazen's Regiment remained in winter camp at Fishkill along the Hudson and north of New York City, Washington, and the main American force continued their march toward the Capital in Philadelphia stopping the last part of December at McConkey's Ferry, on the west bank of the Delaware River. The spot Washington chose was ten miles upstream and on the opposite shore from Trenton, New Jersey, and thirty miles from Philadelphia. This departure from their continued march toward Philadelphia was to prove a pivotal point in American history and the course of the Revolution.

While encampment at McConkey's Ferry, the desperate Washington began to devise a plan. Having no victories to show for his now year and one-half struggle, he knew that he and his forces were near the end if something did not change and change quickly. During this time, he wrote to his cousin in Virginia of his desperation, saying: "I think the game is pretty near up." His army was badly demoralized, starving, and without proper clothing for the coming winter. In addition, more than half of the men in his command would see their enlistments up on December 31.

He had been told by one of his many spies that the Hessian force of 1,500 troops, quartered in Trenton, were in complete disregard for Washington and his ragtag army and consequently could likely be taken by surprise if he decided to attack them.

A week and a half before Christmas, Washington was joined by Lee's army of about 2,000 troops, now commanded by General John Sullivan, after his recent release from British hands, in exchange for British officer Richard Prescott. Washington also welcomed a smaller force commanded by General Horatio Gates, of approximately 800 men. With these additions, his total force, including militia, now numbered a little more than 5,000 with only about half that number healthy enough to take part in what Washington had planned and what he knew would be an extremely difficult task.

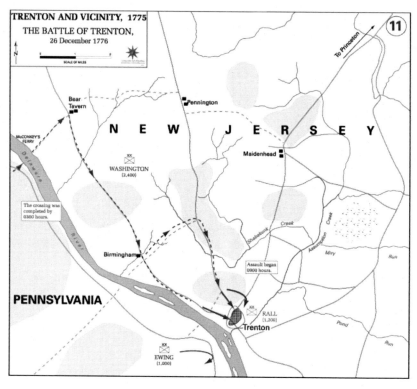

"Battle of Trenton.Dean.USMA.edu.history"
by History Department, United States Military Academy

Beginning at dusk on Christmas Day, Washington and approximately 2,400 troops would cross the Delaware River, ten miles below Trenton, and march the ten miles in sleet and snow to the Hessian compound. Delayed almost three hours by the unbearable weather conditions, his attack would never the less catch the Hessian's by surprise and, in one of the true miracles of the American Revolution, win his first significant battle since forcing the British from Boston. Two-thirds of the Hessian soldiers were either killed, wounded, or were captured, the rest escaping in a rout. American casualties were two dead from exposure on the crossing and the march to Trenton and five wounded during the battle.

Washington's victory at Trenton would be followed up seven days later with a victory over Cornwallis at Assunpink Creek, near Trenton, and the following day with a decisive victory at Princeton. Total casualties for these two days were approximately eighty Americans and three hundred to four hundred British.

Washington now had victories which he could use both to solidify his position as commander in chief and to convince the soldiers, whose enlistment was up, to stay with the army. He also hoped that the victories could be used as a recruiting tool to grow his army.

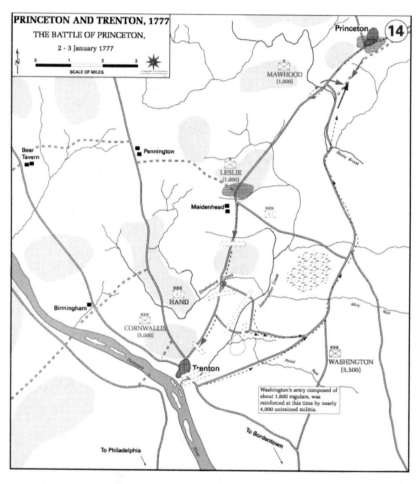

"Battle of Princeton.Dean.USMA.edu.history"
by History Department, United States Military Academy

5

1777—
A REVOLUTION SAVED

FOLLOWING THESE DEFEATS, Cornwallis abandoned most of New Jersey, retreating to New Brunswick, while Washington moved his army north to Morristown, New Jersey, west of New York City where he spent the winter. The American victories raised morale among the troops and throughout the colonies, resulting in thousands of new enlistments in the following months. The terrain surrounding his camp allowed Washington an excellent vantage point from which to keep an eye on the British army, which was headquartered across the Hudson River and south of the city. Washington had also positioned his camp, allowing him to protect the roads leading from the British head-quarters in New York, north to New England, and south toward Philadelphia, the capital of the new United States of America.

Meanwhile, Hazen's Regiment was reorganized on January 1, 1777, and Hazen was allowed to recruit not just from Quebec, but wherever in the Colonies he was able. Hazen's efforts at recruiting met with mixed success as the new states had been assigned quotas to fill for their line companies and they pre-ferred to have men enter their state's units instead of Hazen's.

Hazen's troops remained in camp during the winter months of 1777 as Hazen and Lt. Colonel Edward Antill continued to recruit in order to fill out the ranks of the Regiment. Antill, who was from a distinguished New Jersey family, was very instrumental in helping Hazen recruit, and by late spring, the regiment was at sufficient strength to leave camp and join the main army to which it had been assigned on January 8.

By mid-May, Hazen's regiment had arrived in Princeton, and by August, now part of Sullivan's Division, they were camped at Hanover, New Jersey, where a small skirmish took place prior to the Battle of Staten Island, fought on August 22.

The engagement at Staten Island, although strategically unimportant was tactically a British victory, as the American losses, which were primarily captures, were at least two three times those of the British. Hazen's regimental loss was eight officers and forty men, but the most significant loss was the capture of Lt. Col. Antill, who would not be exchanged until two years later in November 1780.

Following the battle, Sullivan moved his forces south to join Washington in a defensive position along Brandywine Creek.

Washington was convinced that the British main attack would be concentrated at Chad's Ford, but he knew there would be possible attempts at flanking movements to the south or the north. Pyle's Ford, to the south, was thought to be an easily defensible crossing and the only practicable one south of Chad's Ford. Consequently, it was covered by two brigades of Pennsylvania militia to allow the main army to be positioned at Chad's Ford. This point was defended by troops under Nathaniel Greene and General Anthony Wayne. These troops were supported by Thomas Procter's Continental Artillery Regiment.

Major General John Sullivan's force was posted to the right opposite Brinton's Ford about one mile north of Chad's Ford with Major General Lord Stirling's Division in reserve a short distance behind Sullivan. Major General Adam Stephen's

Virginia brigades were also in reserve in a position to move in support of either the right or left of the army.

Three known fords above Brinton's, about two miles apart, were considered the most vulnerable point of the American position and Sullivan was expected to provide adequate cover there. Levan's unit as part of Colonel Moses Hazen's Regiment, now a mixture of new recruits and holdovers from the 2nd Canadian Regiment was detached to cover the upper two known fords to the north of Sullivan's position.

Cavalry was expected to cover the area to the north of Sullivan's position where the creek forked into west and east branches. Unfortunately, a mile further upstream, an east branch ford known as Jeffries' and another on the west branch known as Trimble's left an unguarded route around the American right flank. Washington, usually well informed by his network of spies and locals, was unaware of these critical crossings on his flank, and consequently, Sullivan had not been informed to provide cover at these points. This lack of intelligence and preparation was to be critical in the upcoming battle.

Washington was finally advised of the British flanking movement by Hazen's troops but failed to act on the warning, still convinced that the main attack would come at Chad's Ford. When he was finally convinced in the early afternoon that the main British movement was to his right rear, he began an assault at Chad's Ford but was forced to withdraw.

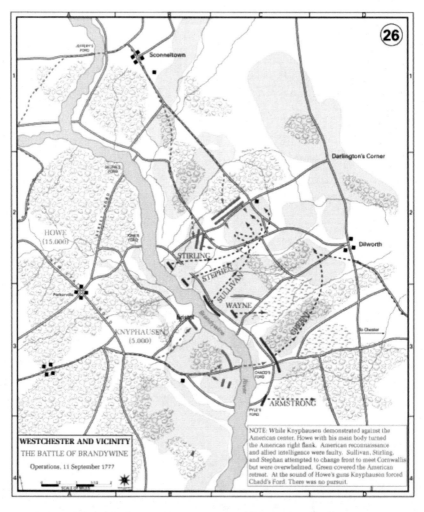

NOTE: While Knyphausen demonstrated against the American center, Howe with his main body turned the American right flank. American reconnaissance and allied intelligence were faulty. Sullivan, Stirling, and Stephan attempted to change front to meet Cornwallis but were overwhelmed. Green covered the American retreat. At the sound of Howe's guns Knyphausen forced Chadd's Ford. There was no pursuit.

WESTCHESTER AND VICINITY

THE BATTLE OF BRANDYWINE

Operations, 11 September 1777

"Battle of Brandywine.Dean.USMA.edu.history"
by History Department, United States Military Academy

Sullivan now aware of the threat on his right and possibly on the rear of some of his forces moved the right wing of the American army to the northeast, meeting the retreating Hazen who had been flanked and forced to abandon his position. Sullivan then consolidated his troops on high ground to meet the British attack.

By this time, convinced by the sound of battle to his right, Washington ordered Greene to move the American forces in reserve to support Sullivan. Arriving too late to prevent Sullivan from being driven from his position by the British attack, Greene and Sullivan were forced to withdraw from the field.

To the south, the British forces at Chad's Ford had mounted an attack across the river on the right flank of the American troops. Driven from their positions all along the Brandywine, the American army, now scattered and confused, withdrew up the road to Philadelphia, leaving the British encamped on the battlefield. With darkness approaching, the Americans were saved from what might have been a disaster.

During the disorganized retreat, Levan had been captivated by a young officer, appearing to be even younger than himself, but dressed as a general officer. The young man passionately was urging the troops to remain steady and orderly as they retreated. As the young officer rode among Hazen's panic-stricken men, Levan turned to his lieutenant.

"Who is that man?"

"I don't know," replied the lieutenant, "but he is seems to be steadying the men."

Just as they spoke, a bullet tore into the young Frenchman's leg, unseating him from his horse. Now down, the young man continued to rally the troops. The bravery of this young man seemed to have a calming effect on the panicked Americans, contributing to what became a more orderly pullback. All of this, before he was treated for his wound.

It would not be the last Levan would see of the Marquis de Lafayette. Over the next few months, the men would discover that the young Frenchman was indeed only days out of his teens and only recently arrived in America. He was to prove himself a young man of both exceptional bravery and ability.

The battle was another stinging defeat for Washington, with a casualty list including wounded and captured numbering 1,000.

Following the battle, Washington led his defeated army north toward Philadelphia, leaving the British camped on the Brandywine field. Washington left behind Smallwood's Maryland Militia and Maj. Gen. Anthony Wayne's Division of Pennsylvania Continentals, to monitor and harass the British Army, on their march to Philadelphia. Wayne camped at a cross-road near a tavern called the General Paoli with Smallwood's militia camped close by. Unfortunately, with men from both armies often frequenting local taverns and the country full of loyalists living in the vicinity, Wayne's encampment and the strength of his force was soon known to Howe, and the British commander was quick to plan an attack to be led by British Major General Grey. The attack, taking place during the night of September 20, completely surprised the encampment as the British attack was made with only the bayonet so the Americans would not be alerted. The British force, holding a 3 to 1 advantage, quickly had the Pennsylvania's in full retreat. As the attack waned, Smallwood's militia rushed toward the Pennsylvanian's camp only to come under attack by the British and to be driven off in confusion, with the American's suffering a second humiliation in less than two weeks. The losses numbered over 200 while the British losses were less than a dozen. Although not of great strategic significance, the Paoli Massacre would be carried in the minds of the Colonists, due to the atrocities carried out by the British, as they reportedly continued to bayonet wounded and surrendering soldiers long after the battle was over.

Levan, in his declaration for pension, offers a brief description of events beginning with his unit's movement from camp towards Brandywine:

> We then left there to Newtons thence to Cooche's ferry in Delaware from thence to Head of Elk. Stayed 2 or 3 weeks from thence to Brandywine and had a battle on 11th day of September 1777. From thence to Paoli, there the enemy came on the men commanded by Genl. Waine (Anthony Wayne) in the night and killed 600 of them by the bayonet.

Unfortunately for the Americans, the humiliation of defeat was to befall them once again before winter would bring the military campaigns of 1777 to a close.

In less than two weeks on October 4, the two armies would once again come to blows and Washington's army would suffer yet another defeat at the hands of Sir William Howe. This time, the Americans were on the offensive instead of the defensive, but the final result was the same. Despite early success in what was a well-designed battle plan, the attack was foiled by the lack of careful execution in carrying out the attack.

The battle took place at the hamlet of Germantown, just northwest of Philadelphia, where Howe had encamped his army after advancing from Brandywine Creek. The battle turned on a mistake by American General Adam Stephen.

Stephen, moving his men to the sound of battle, came upon the rear of Anthony Wayne's forces in a dense fog. Believing that the British troops were before them, Stephen's men fired into their fellow troops.

Wayne's men, fearing that they had been flanked began to fall back in panic, causing the rest of Sullivan's troops to falter.

Washington attempted, without much success, to rally his men, but the attack was now collapsing. The resulting retreat ended what had seemed initially a promising outcome for Washington. As they fell back in retreat, a British reinforcement of three regiments under Cornwallis reached the battlefield but failed to pursue the exhausted Americans and the battle was over. Once again, the losses were devastating for Washington's army as casualties would once again number over 1,000. Losses he could ill afford.

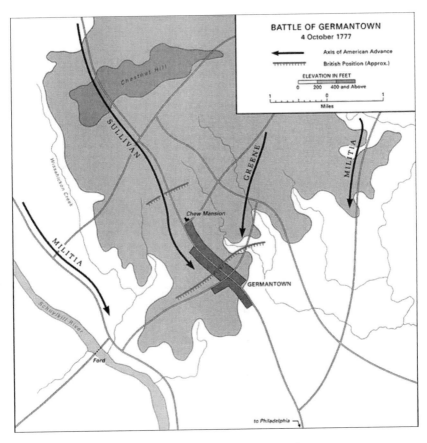

"Battle of Germantown Map"
by U.S. Army Center of Military History Via Wikipedia

Once again Levan describes the Army's movement:

> From thence we went to Germantown and there had a battle on the 11th day of October (actually the 4th). We had to retreat from the enemy but continued about White Marsh 5 or 6 weeks.

Despite the disappointing results over the previous month, there would be good news before year-end. Benedict Arnold and Horatio Gates had crushed General John Burgoyne at Saratoga, in the upper Hudson Valley, surrounded him, and forced him to surrender his command and return with his forces to Canada. The victory at Saratoga was a major turning point in the war as it convinced the French king to reach an alliance with the Americans and to create a global war.

Two months later, in one last attempt to crush Washington's army before the onset of winter, Howe moved his army of approximately 10,000 out of Philadelphia. Howe's intention was to search the battle line Washington had established for an opening or an opportunity to flank. The American forces, now similar in size to those of Howe, had been reinforced by units freed up by the victory at Saratoga and were positioned on high ground near the township of White Marsh. What followed was a disorganized series of skirmishes over a three-day period, as Howe marched and countermarched his forces, searching for the opening he hoped to find. As the British moved back and forth, they took out their frustrations on the civilian population, burning houses and other buildings as they marched.

A German officer serving with the British described the atrocities during the night of December 6:

The sight was horrible. The night was very dark. The blazing flames spread about with all swiftness and the wind blew violently. The cries of human voices of the young and old, who had seen their belongings consumed by the flames without saving anything, put everyone in a melancholy.

Many of those who were in opposition to the Revolution voiced similar shock at the atrocities committed by Howe's soldiers. A young Philadelphia Quaker wrote of their actions in his diary:

Committed great outrages on the inhabitants…as if the sole purpose of the expedition was to destroy and to spread ruin and desolation, to dispose the inhabitants to rebellion by despoiling their property.

On December 7, Howe made one last effort to turn the American flank but was rebuffed and the British withdrew back to Philadelphia.

Washington expressed his disappointment in failing to draw Howe into a more general engagement in a letter to Congress.

I sincerely wish that they had made an Attack; the Issue in all probability, from the disposition of our Troops and the strong situation of our Camp, would have been fortunate and happy. At the same time I must add that reason, prudence, and every principle of policy, forbad us quitting our post to attack them. Nothing but Success would have justified the measure, and this could not be expected from their position.

Before Washington would face the British again in the spring, General Howe would resign his post and return to England, being replaced by Sir Henry Clinton.

Levan describes the action as follows:

> The enemy came on us at White Marsh and we had another engagement. We drove them back and from there we went to winter quarters with Col. Nagles Regt. to the brick meeting house nine miles from Philadelphia. We had been reviewed in Valley Forge by Genl. Miflin in November or December before we went to winter quarters.

6

1778—
A YEAR OF TRANSITION

NOW, WASHINGTON WAS faced with a major decision as to where his troops would stay the winter. He had little choice but to keep them together or to face the task of recruiting a new army in the spring. Asking for suggestions from his generals, Washington received no consensus and he finally settled on Valley Forge.

Valley Forge turned out to be an almost perfect choice. It was west of the city and allowed contact with the Congress now in York and access to the rich farmland of Pennsylvania. Situated on a high plateau protected by the Schuykill River on the north and steep approaches on the south and east, the position offered strong natural defenses against attack.

On December 19, 1777, Washington's army arrived at their destination after an eight-day march from Whitemarsh. The army numbered approximately nine thousand men, many too sick to come to muster. The next few months would be very difficult for everyone, including the commander, who would endure many of the hardships that would face his men. Fortunately, the winter of 1778 was not a harsh one as Pennsylvania winters go, but that good fortune was offset by the lack of provisions, both food and clothing.

A few quotes by those who observed the suffering of the men at Valley Forge:

"An army of skeletons appeared before our eyes naked, starved, sick and discouraged," wrote New York's Gouverneur Morris of the Continental Congress.

The Marquis de Lafayette wrote:

"The unfortunate soldiers were in want of everything; they had neither coats nor hats, nor shirts, nor shoes. Their feet and their legs froze until they were black, and it was often necessary to amputate them."

A bitter George Washington, who's first concern was always his soldiers, would accuse the Congress of

"little feeling for the naked and distressed soldiers. I feel superabundantly for them and from my soul pity those miseries, which it is neither in my power to relieve or prevent."

Washington despaired

"that unless some great and capital change suddenly takes place...this Army must inevitably...starve, dissolve, or disperse, in order to obtain subsistence in the best manner they can."

Although lodged in a home near the one-time ironworks, which gave Valley Forge its name, and not in the roughly constructed log cabins of his men, Washington remained with his soldiers during the winter and worked tirelessly to improve their conditions.

His orders required the construction of the log cabins or huts and even described the style and size. He specified that the huts would be constructed as follows: they would be sixteen by fourteen log huts with six and one-half foot high walls. Each hut was to have a stone fireplace and a wood board roof. The huts were generally built over a two foot deep pit with a dirt floor and a cloth covering over the doorway. The huts, according to Washington's specifications, were to be laid out in such a way to form streets with officer huts to be nearby or behind them. Each hut was to have bunks for twelve men. Those for the officers were to be similar but less crowded. Although Washington's orders called for the close compliance with these rigid specifications, few of the original eight hundred huts met those specifications. Many of the construction flaws only added to the suffering of the soldiers as many of the hastily constructed huts were plagued by improperly placed fireplaces and poor roof construction, both creating unhealthy conditions.

The forest provided for the shelters, but feeding the troops was an entirely different matter. The lack of clothing and food was not due to the lack of availability but sadly due to other reasons.

Primary among these was logistics. Transportation proved a challenge that the Quartermaster General Thomas Miffin was not up to. Not well suited to the job and more interested in personal glorification, Miffin paid little attention to his duties and eventually resigned. A number of factors contributed and compounded this problem. Rain and snow made the roads almost impassable and there was a shortage of teamsters and they were difficult to recruit.

Paper money issued by the Congress was nearly worthless and many of the farmers in the Pennsylvania countryside were reluctant to sell their goods and produce to the army. For the first two months of 1778, conditions at the encampment were horrific. The men, who had little to eat and had very little in the way of warm clothing or shoes, suffered greatly. Hundreds died of disease, made worse by lack of proper diet and clothing. Some estimates of the deaths exceed 2,000 or between 20 and 25 percent of the total force.

Washington worked diligently to improve these conditions, pushing for inoculation against smallpox and for improvements to the sanitary conditions in and around the living quarters. Finally, on March 2, Washington, with assistance from a Congressional committee, convinced his most competent general, Nathanael Greene, to take the position of quartermaster general. Greene and Anthony Wayne led successful foraging expeditions into the countryside, bringing an end to the shortages and thereby boosting the morale of the troops who had endured.

Defenses at Valley Forge had been designed by Washington's chief engineer, French General Louis Duportail. Well conceived, the defensive positions consisted of a line along the top of the ridge facing toward Philadelphia and an inner line around a ridge named Mt. Joy. Troops assigned to these defensive lines were quartered along parallel streets laid out in back of the defenses. If driven from these positions, escape routes had been planned either north across the Schuykill River or west across the Valley Creek.

Soon after Greene began to develop an efficient Quartermaster Organization, a new American army began to take form. In late February, Baron Friedrich Von Steuben arrived at Valley Forge. Although he had served in the Prussian army of Friedrich the

Great, his title was self-bestowed, for he had never risen higher than captain. He had, however, impressed influential members of the new government, including Benjamin Franklin, and he offered to serve without pay if his expenses would be reimbursed.

Washington was immediately impressed by his thoroughness and understanding of the situation, and by late February, he had been appointed inspector general. Von Steuben spoke no English, save for some curse words which he delivered in broken English when displeased. Therefore, he gave his instruction in French through two of Washington's French-speaking aides.

Von Steuben instructed the troops in a hands-on personal manner and expected all junior officers to be able to do the same. This was a new concept to the officer Corp of the Continental Army which had been modeled after the English traditions. He initially trained a core group of a hundred men, the basic company strength, who after achieving proficiency were detailed to take the training to others. By using this method, he soon was able to drill large groups of regimental and brigade strength. The army began to learn how to be an army and how to drill and move in concert on a battlefield.

His instructions stressed the use of the bayonet, a skill the American soldiers had not possessed, but feared in their adversaries, the British, who were masters in the use of it. His instruction included lessons in guard and sentry duty and the need for synchronization of time with the headquarter's clock. He also wrote an army drill manual that was then translated from French into English and copied by an officer in each brigade. The title of the book was *Regulation for the Order of Discipline of the Troops of the United States.*

By late spring, many accomplishments had been achieved by the ragged group which had marched into Valley Forge:

1. For the first time, a large group of men had camped in one place for an extended period.
2. A new Quartermaster Corp had been born, which was the forerunner of today's Quartermaster Corp.
3. The army had truly become a disciplined fighting force using consistent and uniform methods.
4. The formation of a Provost Guard put in place to deal with the many disciplinary issues existing in the army.

In short, a new army had emerged and, when next engaged in battle, would command the respect of the British by performing in an efficient and professional manner never seen before.

Spring brought news that France had entered the war as an ally to the Americans, and more importantly, farmers began bringing their produce to the camp and new uniforms and other military supplies began to arrive. Perhaps most importantly were the new military units arriving, which swelled the ranks of the Continental Army. Morale was also lifted by an extra month of pay for all who had remained and Washington saw to it that a ration of rum was added for each soldier.

On December 21, 1777, Hazen's regiment was ordered to Albany to participate in the planning and execution of an invasion of Canada. The expedition was to be led by the Marquis De Lafayette and Hazen was assigned the position of deputy quartermaster. Planning for the invasion was eventually to be cancelled by problems with supply and staffing.

It is unclear exactly where Isaac Levan spent the Valley Forge months, but his declaration for pension seems to indicate he and his company remained close to the main army and did not accompany the rest of Hazen's regiment to Albany. He indicates, in his declaration, that they went in to winter quarters with Colonel Nagle and did not leave until June.

By June, the American army was ready to move out of its encampment at Valley Forge and resume campaigning against the British. As for the British, General Henry Clinton, who had replaced Sir William Howe, realized that Philadelphia was a difficult place to defend and to make matters worse, the French were now allied with the Americans. He was concerned that he could be facing a blockade by the French fleet or perhaps an attack from both land and sea. For these reasons, Clinton marched his troops out of Philadelphia and back toward New York City, while many of the Philadelphia Tories, soldiers too sick to march, and the baggage were moved by ship.

Washington moved into the Capital City on the heels of the British and quickly began a pursuit of the British Army into New Jersey.

History Department, United States Military Academy

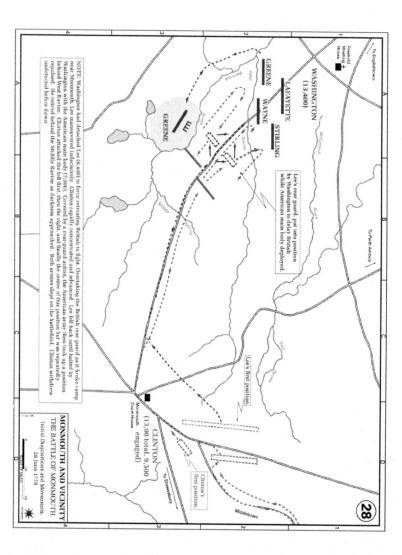

WASHINGTON
(13,400)

GREENE
LAFAYETTE
WAYNE
STIRLING

Freehold
Meeting
House

To Englishtown

To Perth Amboy

Lee's rear guard, put into position
by Washington to delay British
while American main body deployed.

Lee's first position

CLINTON
(13,00 total; 9,500
engaged)

Monmouth
Court House

Clinton's
first position

To Shrewsbury

Middletown

MONMOUTH AND VICINITY
THE BATTLE OF MONMOUTH
Initial Dispositions and Movements,
28 June 1778

NOTE. Washington had detached Lee (6,400) to force retreating British to fight. Overtaking the British rear guard as it broke camp
near Monmouth, Lee maneuvered indecisively. Clinton rapidly concentrated and advanced. Lee fell back until halted by
Washington with the American main body (7,000). Covered by a rear-guard action, the American army then took up a position
behind West Ravine. Clinton attacked the left first, then the right, and finally the center of this position but was repeatedly
repulsed. He retired behind the Middle Ravine as darkness approached. Both armies slept on the battlefield. Clinton withdrew
undetected before dawn.

28

On June 28, 1778, the two armies clashed near Monmouth Court House. A disregard of orders by General Charles Lee prevented an American victory and, except for a counterattack led by an infuriated Washington, might have caused another American defeat.

Washington's bold action prevented a defeat and the American army held the field. Later, Lafayette reflecting on Washington at Monmouth observed: "I thought then as now I had never beheld so superb a man."

Again, Levan offers his perspective on the battle: "In this battle both armies retreated. Genl. Lee commanded the left wing and gave orders to retreat wrongfully as the enemy was retreating at the same time."

In a letter written to his brother John after the battle, Washington gives his perspective of the event:

> The Enemy evacuated Philadelphia on the 18th. Instt. at ten o'clock that day I got intelligence of it, and by two o'clock, or soon after, had Six Brigades on their March for the Jerseys, and followed with the whole Army next Morning…moved down towards the Enemy, and on the 27th, got within Six Miles of them.
>
> General Lee having the command of the Van of the Army, consisting of fully 5000 chosen Men, was ordered to begin the Attack next Morning so soon as the enemy began their March, to be supported by me. But, strange to tell! when he came up with the enemy, a retreat commenced; whether by his order, or from other causes, is now the subject of inquiry, and consequently improper to be descanted on, as he is in arrest, and a Court Martial sitting for tryal of him. A Retreat however was the fact, be the causes as they may; and the disorder arising from it

would have proved fatal to the Army had not that bountiful Providence which has never failed us in the hour of distress, enabled me to form a Regiment or two (of those that were retreating) in the face of the Enemy, and under their fire, by which means a stand was made long enough (the place through which the enemy were pursuing being narrow) to form the Troops that were advancing, upon an advantageous piece of Ground in the rear; hence our affairs took a favourable turn, and from being pursued, we drove the Enemy back, over the ground they had followed us, recovered the field of Battle, and possessed ourselves of their dead. but, as they retreated behind a Morass very difficult to pass, and had both Flanks secured with thick Woods, it was found impracticable with our Men fainting with fatigue, heat, and want of Water, to do anything more that Night. In the Morning we expected to renew the Action, when behold the enemy had stole off as Silent as the Grave in the Night after having sent away their wounded. Getting a Nights March of us, and having but ten Miles to a strong post, it was judged inexpedient to follow them any further, but move towards the North River least they should have any design upon our posts there.

He continued the letter with additional information on casualties on both sides and the need for additional troops. He ended the letter:

"As the Post waits I shall only add my love to my Sister and the family, and Strong assurances of being with the Sincerest regard and Love, Yr. most Affect. Brother."

Although considered a draw, the Battle of Monmouth saw something new in the war: a retreat by the British. Monmouth was the last major battle in the northern theater of the American struggle for independence, as the major conflict would soon shift to the South.

As a result of his failures at Monmouth, Lee was later court-martialed, found guilty, and removed from command.

Levan's declaration provides details on the next movement of Washington's army:

> From there we marched to the state of Connecticut and stayed in Fredericksburg till in November and then went to Middlebrook and Boundbrook. Washington had his headquarters on Raritan River. The Pennsylvanians had theirs between Raritan River and Millstone River.

Following Monmouth, the British continued eastwards until they reached Sandy Hook where they were taken by boat to New York City. The French fleet under the command of Vice Admiral D'Estaing narrowly missed trapping Clinton's army at Sandy Hook, but arrived too late. The British expected an attack on New York and immediately began preparation against a combined American-French attack, but those plans were abandoned by Washington and D'Estaing. New York remained in British hand until 1783.

7

1779—
A NEW AMERICAN ARMY

WASHINGTON KNEW HIS army needed to change in order to compete with the strict discipline exhibited by his adversaries, both British and Hessian. During his service alongside the British during the French and Indian War, he had seen how the discipline among the British troops improved all facets of military life. Less than two weeks after his appointment as commander in chief, he had petitioned the Continental Congress for the authority to appoint a provost marshal. His request was approved and by the following General Order, the first provost marshal of the Continental Army was appointed.

Headquarters, Cambridge, January 10, 1776

His Excellency, General Washington, has been pleased to appoint Mr. William Marony, provost marshal to the Army of the United Colonies, serving in the Massachusetts Bay; he is, therefore, in all things appertaining to his office, to be considered and obeyed as such.

Washington wrote the following personal note to Marony, a sergeant in the Massachusetts troops, advising him of the appointment and responsibilities:

All persons guilty of capital crimes and crimes not triable by a regimental court-martial are to be sent to the provost.

The provost is not to receive any prisoner without a crime specified in writing and signed by the person committing him. No prisoner is to be suffered to be absent from his confinement until released by proper authority.

The provost marshal is to provide a suitable person, when necessary, to execute the sentences of general courts-martial approved of and directed to be enforced by the Commander in Chief.

When any men are sent to the provost, the provost marshal is to send a report of them immediately to the regiment they belong to; and no man is to be received by the provost unless his crime is sent with him.

The provost is to make a return every morning by ten o'clock, to the adjutant general, of the numberof prisoners under guard, specifying the regiments they belong to, their crimes, by whom, and how long confined.

The provost is to take due care that all orders from the judge advocate respecting the trials of prisoners

be punctually executed and is to post proper sentries from his guard, at such times and in such places as a general court-martial may sit.

The provost is frequently to take a party from his guard and patrol the avenues and environs of the camp, is to take up and confine all disorderly and suspicious persons, to suppress riots and disturbances, and to inform the quartermaster general of all persons who keep unwarranted and destructive dram shops and all other pernicious and camp nuisances.

The provost is to receive and obey all such orders and instructions as may, at any time, be given him by his Excellency the Commander in Chief, the adjutant general, the quartermaster general, and the judge advocate of the Army of the United Colonies.

The provost marshal was primarily a jailer but had the authority to use the provost guards assigned to him to perform the function of military police. During the next two years, discipline improved but still fell short of what the commander in chief expected.

Marony, after his own desertion, was followed by a series of replacements, none of them performing to the level expected by Washington. A portion of this failure was due to lack of support for the provost guard itself and to the limited number of men assigned to this duty.

Washington continued to petition for an improved provost guard, and in November of 1777, he received a letter that would significantly change the situation with regard to military authority.

The letter was from Captain Bartholomew Von Heer, who had served in the Continental Army, beginning with the Canadian Regiment under Livingston, and later Hazen until March of 1777. At that time, he was appointed captain of a company in the Pennsylvania State Artillery, under the command of Colonel Thomas Proctor. He was serving in that capacity when he wrote Washington and volunteered his service in the establishment of a mounted military police unit, referred to in Europe as the Marechaussee.

A Representation to the Commander in Chief of the American Army

The Commander in Chief I understand he was informed by a certain Noble Gentleman in the Army that it was of great necessity of the good of the American Army and for the publick of the United States of America to raise a Core of Marishusy which as such Core is used in every power in Europe in time of War and Peace to support the publick and the Army as I have the honour to inform his Excellency that enquiring was been made if there was any Outland Officer in the Army which was well acquainted with that office of Marishusy he should be applied for that purpose.

I have the honour to inform his Excellency that I am an Officer which is acquainted with such duty in time being several year in the service of his Majestys the Kings of Prussia France and Spain in peace and war time in the Horse as well as Infantry in which time I have seen and learned this duty as a Marishusy and flatter myself to his Excellency that I can give instruction of such Office as well as any Officer which is acquainted with such Core.

A Representation to the Commander in Chief of the American Army —

The Commander in Chief Understood, he was Informed by a certain Noble Gentleman in the Army that it was of great Necessity of the Good of the American Army and for the Publick of the United States of America to Raise a Core of Marishay which as such Core is used in every power in Europe in time of Warr and peace to Support the Publick and the Army as I have the Honour to Inform his Excellency that Enquiring was been made if there was any Outland Officer in the army which was well acquainted with that Office of Marishay he should be applied for that purpose —

I have the Honour to Inform his Excellency that I am an Officer which is Acquainted with such duty in time being several Years in the Service of his Majesties the Kings of Prussia France and Spain in peace and Warr Servd in the Horse as well as Infantry in which time I have seen and Learned this Duty as a Marishay and flatter myself to his Excellency that I can give Instruction of such Officer as well as any Officer which is Acquainted with such a Core —

Von Heer to Washington November 17, 1777

The letter continued with an explanation of specific duties and the makeup of the Corp. The Marechaussee Corps as described by Von Heer would be made up as follows:

1 Commander
1 Captain
4 Lieutenants
1 Quartermaster, to draw provisions.
1 Clerk to keep an exact book of all transactions of the service
2 Trumpeters to give proper notices
2 Sergeants
5 Corporals one assigned to each officer
43 Privates on horseback
4 Negroes to perform the executions

It is safe to say that Washington was impressed with the letter from Von Heer and with his service to his adopted country, as well as the recommendations from others of Von Heer's qualifications.

On January 29, 1778, Washington, in a long letter to a Congressional Camp Committee, stated the need for a major reorganization of the Continental Army to include the establishment of Provost Corps. He required the men of the Provost to be assigned as light dragoons and they must be trustworthy above all else. These men were to receive higher pay and there was to be a higher ratio of officers to enlisted men, and their assignment was to, in Washington's words, "watch over the good order and regularity of the army."

Washington continued to push for the formation of the Corps during the months at Valley Forge, and on May 27,

1778, the Continental Congress authorized the Corps and defined its role:

> "Their business was to watch over the regularity and good order of the army in camp, quarters, or on the march, quell riots, prevent marauding, straggling and desertions, detect spies, regulate sutlers and the like."

When notified of the Corps approval, Von Heer began to put together his new command.

They came primarily from troops serving in Pennsylvania units, and when completed, the unit was almost entirely German, with many speaking only their native tongue. Recruiting men of German ethnicity helped in forming a unit that proved to be a more cohesive one as time wore on.

On July 27, 1778, Washington wrote his new provost commander the following letter:

To Captain Bartholomew von Heer
Head Quarters White Plains 27 July 1778

Sir.

Upon receiving this letter you are immediately to repair to camp to the exercise of the duties of your office—There is no useful purpose answered that I know of by your absence, while the advantages of the institution are in a great measure lost to the army.

If you have procured cloathing for your corps, it may be directed to be sent on after you.

I am Sir your obt hble servt.

After the battle of Monmouth, Washington's army moved to the north, positioning itself to guard the Hudson River against any movement north, by the British Army in New York City.

With the approach of winter, Washington had another decision to make, where to position his troops for the winter in order to protect New Jersey, to pose a threat to the British in New York and Staten Island, and to be in a position to quickly advance north should the British threaten a movement down the Hudson.

He chose Middlebrook, a small New Jersey village in Somerset County, as the spot for the main portion of his army. Smaller forces were positioned near Elizabethtown, guarding the coast and at Danbury, Connecticut, where a move toward the highlands, or south toward Manhattan, could be made.

Once again, Washington's troops would be blessed with a rather mild winter and, in contrast with the previous year at Valley Forge, would have much better support in terms of food and clothing, due to the efforts of General Greene. There were periodic shortages, but the men did not starve and freeze as they had the previous winter.

As at Valley Forge, Washington ordered construction of standardized housing similar to those built the previous year. Again, his choice of camp location provided more than adequate materials from the surrounding forests for their needs.

The formation of the provost unit would be of great significance to Isaac Levan, for while in winter quarters between the Raritan and Millstone Rivers, Levan's enlistment in Hazen's regiment ended as indicated in the following excerpt from his declaration.

Here I was discharged on the third day of March 17th 1779 by Captain Sealy by order of Genl. Hazen. I then enlisted again the same day after my discharge a Dragoon for three years more under Capt Bartholomew Van Heer. The regiment was called Marechausee. The first lieutenant was Phillip Manke–the second lieutenant was Jacob Menninger–the coronet was Baron Wolfin. We had no Col. over us only as they was appointed at different times to muster us. The first of them was Col. Stuart of the second regiment of the Pennsylvania troops in the town of Redding—while in winter quarters. We marched from Raritan River in the spring of 1779 in April or May to Smith's Clove. Washington had his headquarters there by Smith's Tavern.

The staff that Levan would now report to was First Lieutenant Jacob Mytinger and Second Lieutenant Philip Strubing.

The sergeants were Franz Harker, George Hess, and John Mutter and the trumpeters, Lewis Wolf and John George.

The corporals were David Erskine, John Effinger, Anthony Wachter, Jacob Shafer, and Philip Smith.

Many of these many would serve with Levan throughout his service.

In late May, British General Clinton moved north out of New York City, with a force of several thousand in hopes of drawing Washington out of the highlands, onto terrain where he hoped to defeat the Americans and put and end to the rebellion. Supported by the British Navy, he moved up the Hudson with the objective of capturing the small fortresses at Stony Point and Fort Lafayette, on the east side of the river at Verplanck's Point, and the strategic ferry connecting the two. Once in control of the river to this point, Clinton hoped to mount an attack north on West Point, which was considered the key to controlling the Hudson. His forces easily captured both forts, each manned with less than 100 troops and he immediately began to strengthen both fortifications. Washington, learning of Clinton's movement began to break camp in May and move his army to the north above New York City, just west of the Hudson River near present-day Monroe, New York, then called Smith's in the Clove. Washington's Headquarters were at nearby Smith's Tavern. From this point, he expected to be able to confront Clinton and to disrupt his plans to seize control of the Hudson.

Levan and the rest of Von Heer's command was a part of this movement and were to camp at Smith's in the Clove. On June 2, while encamped at the Clove, Von Heer received orders from Washington through his aide-de-camp, Richard K. Meade, to send a noncommissioned officer with four dragoons to an encampment of the Virginia Division.

> To Major General Arthur St. Clair
> Head Quarters, June 2, 1779.
>
> I have ordered a Non Commissioned officer and eight Dragoons from the Marechaussie corps to join you immediately at I send you a little sketch that will serve to give you an idea of the country you are in, I am, yos

That same day he was instructed by James McHenry, an aide to General Washington, to "dispatch one half of the horse now with you, light and unencumbered of baggage to join the party sent yesterday to General St. Clair."

Upon receipt of the order, Von Heer quickly selected Lt. Mytinger and provided him a copy of the order. Mytinger quickly went about picking the men he would take, including

Levan. Once he had selected the three noncommissioned officers and twenty privates, he gathered the group to give them their orders.

"You men, mount up. Take as little as you can for you will be provided with your requirements when we reach St Clair's force."

General St. Clair was on the march from Pompton, New Jersey, and the detachment was to support Sr. Clair and screen for his force.

On June 6, Washington again sent orders to General St. Clair instructing him to be careful in seeing that his line of march was not compromised.

To Major General Arthur St. Clair
Head Quarters, June 6, 1779.

Sir: There is a road leading from Kings ferry to Junes through the Mountains, by which it is possible the enemy may intercept our line of march. You will be pleased to send a good subaltern and a party down that road to send his patroles as near the enemy as he can with safety and communicate the earliest intelligence of any movement. You will for this purpose furnish him with a few horse. If some of the inhabitants well affected and acquainted with the country can be engaged to accompany the party, it will be very useful. It is not improbable there may be parties of the militia on the same road. The officer that commands your party should be cautioned against mistakes. I am, etc.

Levan and his fellow Dragoons joined St. Clair on the march and continued with him until they arrived at Galloway's in Smith's Clove. There, the Dragoons received their orders and took up camp with St. Clair's troops. They remained there for three weeks before being ordered to march over the mountains to West Point. At West Point, they joined the troops of General Alexander McDougall, who commanded the garrisons there. They were placed under the direction of Colonel Tadeusz Kościuszko, who had been assigned the responsibility for defensive improvements to Forts Clinton and Putnam. These fortifications, located next to the river and on the hill above, were strategically positioned to control high ground surrounding West Point on both sides of the river and a chain was placed across the river to prevent access up the river by boat.

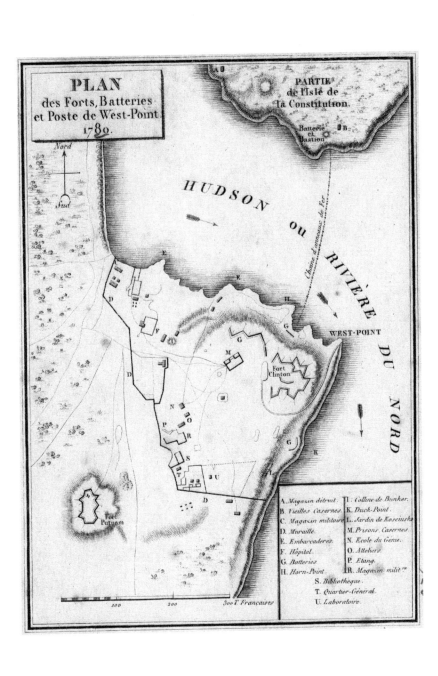

PLAN
des Forts, Batteries
et Poste de West-Point.
1780.

Nord

Sud

PARTIE
de l'Isle de
la Constitution.

Batterie
et
Bastion

HUDSON ou RIVIÈRE DU NORD

WEST-POINT

Chaîne d'anneaux de Fer

Fort Clinton

Fort Putnam

A. Magasin détruit.
B. Vieilles Casernes.
C. Magasin militaire.
D. Muraille.
E. Embarcaderes.
F. Hôpital.
G. Batteries.
H. Horn-Point.
I. Colline de Bunker.
K. Duck-Point.
L. Jardin de Kosciusko.
M. Prisons, Casernes.
N. Ecole du Génie.
O. Ateliers.
P. Etang.
R. Magasin milit.re
S. Bibliothèque.
T. Quartier-Général.
U. Laboratoire.

100   200   300 T. Francaises

During this effort, the men of Levan's company helped place an array of sunken logs, called a chevaux-de-frise, in the river to supplement the chain placed previously.

GREAT CHAIN AND MORTARS.

From Levan's declaration:

"From here we was sent down Smith's river five miles to Genl. Sinclair as a front guard of the army. Stayed about three weeks then marched over the mountains to west point on north river. Here we built two forts. The one next the river was called Putnam the other was on the hill. (Author's note: Ft. Clinton (Ft. Arnold) was near the river and Putnam was above on the hill—see map) Here we put in the river a Chevaux-Defrise. At this place we had to patrol from fort Putnam to Stony Point every day."

In addition to assisting in the ongoing improvements to the defenses, as mounted troops, they made daily patrols down the river toward Stony Point and to the west, on trails leading toward the main road leading north from Kings Ferry, toward

Smith's Clove. The patrols were to ensure that Clinton made no unseen movement toward the main American army at the Clove or on West Point.

Reconnaissance reports, from these patrols and other sources including his network of spies, allowed Washington to be aware of any movement Clinton might make with regard to his positions on the Hudson. These surveillances allowed Washington to be ready when Clinton began to withdraw part of his force in late June, and the general began to formulate plans of his own.

During the first week of July, the main British force was transported by ship to the Connecticut coast, where Clinton began a series of weeklong raids beginning at New Haven on July 5 and ending at Norwalk on July 11.

This withdrawal left between six hundred and seven hundred British regulars and a detachment from a regiment of American loyalists, commanded by Colonel Henry Johnson at Stony Point, and a similar garrison on the opposite side of the river at Verplanck's Point.

Levan in the meantime had seen his assignment changed once more.

On the morning of July 2, Von Heer had received orders from Washington, to assign a dragoon to Anthony Wayne to serve as an orderly so that he might keep in close contact with his recently promoted commander.

Later that day, Lt. Mytinger, who had been given the responsibility of assigning a man to that duty, approached Levan.

"Levan," he barked. "Get yourself a mount, gather up your gear, draw powder and shot as well as some rations. You are to report to General Wayne at Fort Montgomery and serve him as orderly until you receive further orders."

"Yes sir," Levan replied.

Levan collected his gear, drew a ration of powder and shot, and was soon on his way downriver to Fort Montgomery, where he arrived midafternoon. Upon arriving, he was quickly directed to General Wayne's headquarters where he was met by one of Wayne's aides.

"Soldier, what is your business here?"

"My commander, Captain Von Heer, sent me here on orders of General Washington to serve as orderly to General Wayne," replied Levan.

"Yes, I believe the general did mention that General Washington had indicated he would do so," said the aide. "I will let the general know you are here. What is your name?"

"Levan, sir, Isaac Levan."

"Do you have a tent?" questioned the officer.

"No, sir, I was not able to bring a tent."

"Very well, we will see you have a place to sleep and get you situated and some grain for your horse. You will need to be quartered near the general's headquarters, but first, let me introduce you to the general. Come with me."

The officer motioned Levan to follow him and they walked a few hundred feet to a large house, around which the army was camped. Entering the home, they found Wayne seated at a desk in a front room, writing what could only be dispatches or orders.

"General sir, this soldier has been sent from headquarters by General Washington to serve you as orderly. He is a member of Von Heer's Dragoons. His name is Isaac Levan. He is German, but his English is quite good."

"Come in, soldier," said Wayne, "have a seat and let us talk."

Over the next few minutes, Wayne outlined what he expected of Levan and what he himself could expect while attached to his service.

The general told Levan that he had been making some reconnaissances and that they would do so the next morning.

With that, Levan was dismissed and began the effort of settling in to his new surroundings.

Fort Montgomery
July 3, 1779

As Wayne had indicated, early the next morning, the two men, along with other members of Wayne's staff and a small escort of cavalry, were off to check on the activities at Stony Point.

Arriving at a promontory, which Levan later learned was a place called Buckberg Mountain, they found themselves in a perfect position to observe the river below and the main objects of interest, Kings Ferry and Stony Point. The men observed a bustle of activity, as the British troops went about the reinforcing and rebuilding of the earthen works located there. From their vantage point, it was easy for Wayne to see that an attack on those fortifications would be no easy task. Although not a fort in the truest sense of the word, Stony Point was well appointed with other obstacles, which would make any effort to conquer it a difficult job at the very least. The defenses consisted of earthen works, where cannons could be positioned and a network of trees sharpened to a point and placed in the earthen embankments, commonly referred to as abatis. These earthen defenses set atop a rocky elevation facing west, the only direction from which they could be approached. They were further protected in the front by a narrow watery gorge and on both flanks by large swampy areas.

After taking note of the significant features of their objective and assessing as best they could the number of defenders, the men continued their ride. As they rode, they made observations of anything deemed significant on the terrain through which they passed with notations, made by the general's aides.

Fort Montgomery
July 4, 1779

The next morning, Levan was called to Wayne's headquarters and given a dispatch by one of the general's staff.

"Soldier, this dispatch is to be delivered to General Washington himself and no one else. I should not have to tell you that any written correspondence between the two generals you may be given to deliver must be protected at all costs."

The dispatch included their observations of the day before and held a sketch of the area drawn by either Wayne or one of his staff.

Levan hurriedly choked down what breakfast was available, saddled and mounted his horse, and rode off to West Point, a ride of some three miles. Arriving there, Levan discovered that Washington had not come down to West Point but was still at his headquarters in New Windsor. Quickly back in the saddle, Levan rapidly covered the seven- or eight-mile ride from West Point, to New Windsor, and was soon escorted by a young lieutenant to the home of Colonel Thomas Ellison, where Washington had made his headquarters. Arriving at the home, the escort asked the guard posted at the door to summon a member of the general's staff.

Presently, the guard returned. With him was a young man who Levan perceived to be not much older than him. This assessment proved to be accurate, as it was Lieutenant Colonel

Alexander Hamilton, Washington's aide-de-camp, who came to see who was calling upon the General. Hamilton was in his early twenties and only months older than Levan.

"What is this man's business?" Hamilton asked the young escort.

"He says he has been sent from General Wayne with a dispatch he was told to deliver only in the presence of the general himself."

"Is that correct, soldier?"

"Yes, sir, the general said it was for General Washington only and important that it not fall into the wrong hands."

"Do you fear that mine could be the wrong hands?"

"No, sir, it's only that the general himself ordered me directly."

"I understand and I commend your attention to your orders. I will let the general know you are here."

Hamilton reentered the house, and within only a few minutes, he returned and after dismissing the escort, motioned for Levan to follow him inside.

"Follow me," he said.

Levan stepped into the entrance and was immediately directed to a large front room off the main hallway. Here he observed an officer seated at a desk from which there was both a view of the door and a window, from which he could observe the steps leading to the porch from which Levan had waited.

As Levan entered, the man stood and turned toward him. He was a very imposing figure, a giant of a man to Levan, who stood only about five and one-half feet.

In a gesture Levan thought unusual for the circumstances, given the distinct difference in station, Washington extended a huge hand and welcomed Levan.

"I understand you have a dispatch from General Wayne and that you wish to deliver it to me directly," Washington said in a very authoritative voice.

"Yes, sir, those were the orders he gave me."

"Well then, I congratulate you on your observance to duty as I am the man you seek. What is your name soldier?" the general continued.

"Levan, sir, Isaac Levan."

"I see you are dressed as a Marechaussee. Were you posted with Wayne by Captain Von Heer? Is the Marechaussee your first service?"

"Yes, sir, I was ordered by the captain to serve as orderly to General Wayne. I joined the Marechaussee in the spring after serving with General Hazen for three years."

"Have you seen battle?" Washington asked.

"Yes, sir, at Quebec, Brandywine, Germantown, and Monmouth."

"Very commendable, young man, most do not remain as devoted to their duty and our cause. You are very young, do you have family?"

"No, sir, I am in America for six years. What little family I have is still in Germany. I came alone when I was seventeen."

"Very well," Washington replied. "Let's see what you have for me."

Levan handed Washington the dispatch and stood quietly at attention as the general broke the seal and began to read.

Noticing Levan's stiff stance, Washington spoke.

"At ease, soldier. Hamilton, see that he gets something to eat and a place to rest until I have finished General Wayne's letter. I am sure I will have a response that young Levan can take back to the general."

Levan was led to a room with a large table in the center, which he took as the family dining room. A young woman, who Levan assumed was a servant, offered him some bread and cheese and a selection of sweet rolls which were displayed on the table. On a small serving table to the side, there was a pitcher of cider and a bottle of port. He accepted bread and cheese and a cup of the cider and took a chair at a small table where he ate and waited for a response to his dispatch.

Meanwhile, Washington continued to read Wayne's dispatch, commenting on it, and the sketch to his aides who stood behind him.

Finishing Wayne's report, Washington withdrew some blank paper from a stack on his desk and began to write.

> To B. Gen. Wayne Commanding Light Infantry
> Headquarters July 4th 1779
>
> Dear Sir,
>
> This morning I received Your letter of yesterday and am obliged to you for your observations and the sketch you sent me.
>
> The arrival of the southern Post expected tomorrow will detain me here; but the next day I shall have the pleasure of being with you very early in the morning for the purpose you mention. You may make a disposition of your Corps as you think proper.
>
> I am Dear Sir, ys.
>
> G. Washington

When he finished, Washington summoned Levan and handed him the sealed letter, which he placed in the dispatch pouch. A short time later, he was retracing his route of the morning, back to Fort Montgomery.

When he arrived at Wayne's headquarters, he delivered the dispatch and turned to leave. As he moved away, Wayne motioned for him to stay.

"Wait," he said. "I may have further use of you."

After finishing Washington's letter, he spoke up.

"That will be all, Levan. Stay close, I may have need of you before the day is done."

The day passed without further incident and the next day as well, until after the evening meal when he was summoned to Wayne's office.

"It seems General Washington will be paying us a visit early tomorrow morning. Be ready to ride with us when the general arrives."

Fort Montgomery
July 6, 1779

As expected, Washington arrived at Fort Montgomery early on the morning of July 6 and joined Wayne, Levan, and a group of escorts, for a morning reconnaissance back to Buckberg Mountain. Through a telescope, they could clearly observe the ongoing construction of fortifications at the Point and they began to consider how they might plan an assault on the British position there.

Returning to headquarters at New Windsor, Washington began to put together all the information and observations he had been provided and to develop a plan that he felt would have the best chance of succeeding against what seemed to be a very formidable position.

8

STONY POINT

ON THE NINTH day of July, Washington wrote Wayne the following letter, making it clear that he wished him to hasten his preparations to attack Stony Point.

New Windsor, July 9, 1779.

Dr Sir:

While the enemy are making excursions to distress the country it has a very disagreeable aspect to remain in a state of inactivity on our part. The reputation of the army and the good of the service seem to exact some attempt from it. The importance of Stoney Point to the enemy makes it infinitely desireable that could be the object. The works are formidable; but perhaps on a fuller examination they may be found accessible. A deserter yesterday informed me there was a sandy beach on the South side running along the flank of the works and only obstructed by a slight abbatis which might afford an easy and safe approach to a body of troops.

I wish you to take every step in your power to ascertain this and to gain a more accurate knowledge of the position in general, particularly, on the flanks and in the rear. Would it answer to send in a trusty intelligent fellow from you in character of a deserter, on some plan that might enable him to return with expedition?

I beg you to inform yourself all you can, and to give me your opinion of the practicability of an attempt upon this post.

If it is undertaken, I should conceive it ought to be done by way of surprise in the night. I am, etc.

The very next day, he again wrote Wayne from his headquarters at New Windsor, outlining some of his ideas for the attack. It is clear from this letter that Washington was an excellent military strategist and left little to chance when planning operations in advance.

"My ideas of the Enterprise in contemplation are these: that it should be attempted by the Light Infantry only, which should march under cover of night and with the utmost secrecy to the Enemy's lines, securing every person they find, to prevent discovery. Between one and two hundred chosen men and officers I conceive fully sufficient for the surprise; and apprehend the approach should be along the Water on the South side, crossing the Beach and entering at the abatis…This party is to be preceded by a Vanguard of prudent and determined men, well commanded, who are to remove obstructions, secure the sentries, and drive in the guards. They are to advance the whole of them with fixed Bayonets and muskets unloaded…These parties should be followed by the main body at a small distance, for the purpose of support and making good the advantages which may be gained, or to bring them off in case of repulse and disappointment…

The Three approaches here mentioned should be well reconnoitered beforehand, and by persons of observation... Secrecy is so much more essential to these kind of enterprises, than numbers, that I should not think it advisable to employ any other than the light troops. If a surprize takes place, they are fully competent to the business; if it does not, numbers will avail little. As it is in the power of a single Deserter to betray the design, defeat the project...A knowledge of your intention, ten minutes previously obtained, will blast all your hopes; for which reason a small detachment, composed of men whose fidelity you can rely on, under the care of a Judicious Officer, should guard every avenue through the marsh to the Enemy's works...The usual time for exploits of this kind is a little before day, for which reason a vigilant officer is then more on the watch. I therefore recommend a midnight hour... These are my general ideas of the plan for a surprize; but you are at liberty to depart from them in every instance, where you may think they may be improved, or changed for the better. A Dark night, and even a rainy one, (if you can find the way,) will contribute to your success...As it is a part of the plan, if the surprize should succeed, to make use of the enemy's Cannon against their shipping and their post on the other side, it will be well to have a small detachment of artillery with you to serve them. I have sent an order to the park for this purpose, and, to cover the design, have ordered down a couple of light field-pieces. When you march, you can leave the pieces behind. So soon as you have fixed your plan and the time of execution, I shall be obliged to you to give me notice. I shall immediately order you a reinforcement of light Infantry and Espontoons.

New Windor
July 14, 1779

Five days later, Washington again wrote Wayne, ordering him to put their plan into execution, unless Wayne felt otherwise advised. In the letter, he indicated that he had reflected on the advantages and disadvantages of delaying the proposed attack and determined that he was in favor of proceeding. Washington's letter stated:

> "You will therefore carry it into execution tomorrow night, as you desired, unless some new motive or better information should induce you to think it best to defer it."

Fort Montgomery
July 15, 1779

On the morning of the fifteenth, Wayne sent a letter to Washington, indicating that he had made further reconnaissance and had decided to proceed with the attack. The letter is very optimistic regarding the outcome.

> On the 11th Colonels Butler(9th Pennsylvania)and Febiger (2nd Virginia) with myself reconnoitered the enemies works at Stoney Point in the most satisfactory manner feasible and are decidedly of opinion that two real attacks and one faint ought to be made agreeable to the enclosed plan disposition which I now do myself the honor to transmit. By the unanimous voice of the field officers present as well as by your Excellencies per-

mission, I have ventured to add the second attack which is the only alteration from your's of the tenth...I perfectly agree with your Excellency that an enterprise of this nature doesn't so much depend upon numbers as on secrecy & prowess.

He closed the letter on the following note of optimism:

I am pleased with the prospect of the day and have the most happy presages of the fortunes of the night.

Adieu my Dear General and believe me
with every Sentiment of esteem
Your most ob and affectionate

Hum. Ser.
Ant. Wayne

After penning the letter, Wayne mustered his forces and they began their march from Fort Montgomery beginning at midday. As they proceeded, they were careful to detain any civilians they met to ensure they did not warn the British of their intentions. Instead of a more direct line of approach, they moved farther to the west, often forced to make their way in a single file. Their chosen approach took them over the roughest of terrains on roads that were mere cart or foot paths. About 8 p.m., the first troops began arriving at a farm a mile and one half from their objective.

Wayne's Route of March to Stony Point Dean_USMA_edu_history

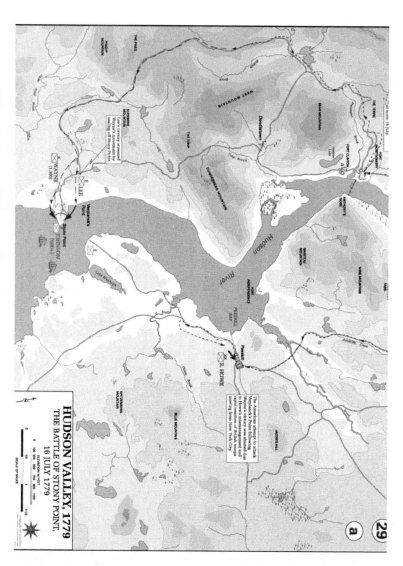

Wayne's movement to Stony Point. Lee's cavalry screened Wayne's movement by sealing off Stony Point.

The American attempt to attack Verplanck's Point following Wayne's victory was aborted due to Howe's mismanagement and rapid reaction of British troops moving from New York City.

HUDSON VALLEY 1779
THE BATTLE OF STONY POINT,
16 JULY 1779

ELEVATION IN FEET
0   100 200   500   800 1000

SCALE OF MILES
0   1/2   1/2

29

a

By 10 p.m. they were formed up into three attack columns, consisting of two flanking and one in the center. The center force was tasked with creating a diversion or feint, as Washington had called it in his letter to Wayne of July 9. The column on the north side was to be commanded by Colonel Butler of the 9th Pennsylvania, with unloaded muskets and bayonets fixed. The main force on the south was to be commanded by Wayne, with Lieutenant Colonel Francois Louis Teisseydre, Marquis de Fleury leading the first wave and also ordered to use only the bayonet. Both flanking forces were to be led forward by a body of twenty men who had volunteered for the most hazardous duty. They had been dubbed the "forlorn hope" and were to be led by Lt. James Gibbons and Lt. George Knox, respectively. Gibbons and Knox had been chosen by lot, from a group of officers who had all volunteered to lead the "forlorn hope." Their mission was to use axes and picks, which they carried in addition to their muskets, to break holes in the fortifications, allowing the men who followed to pass through unimpeded. The center column, commanded by Major Hardy Murfree, a North Carolinian, was the only force to approach with loaded muskets.

Before moving out to their assigned points of attack, each of the men was issued a ration of rum and given their orders. In addition, they each were given a piece of white paper to be attached to their hat, in order for them to be distinguished from the enemy, in the darkness.

Once again, as happened frequently during their fight for freedom, providence blessed them, as high winds forced the supporting British ships to move downriver to a safer mooring and clouds increasing the darkness of the night, sheltered their advance.

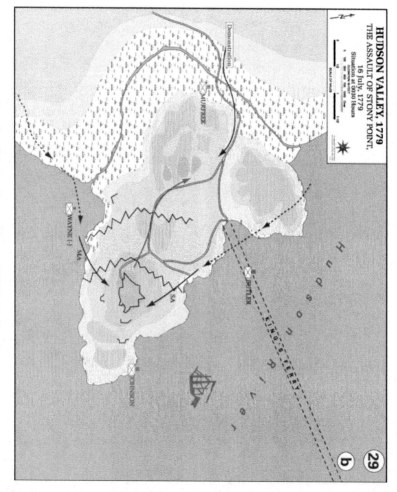

HUDSON VALLEY, 1779
THE ASSAULT OF STONY POINT,
16 July, 1779
Situation at 0030 Hours
ELEVATION IN FEET

SCALE OF MILES

Battle of Stony Point Dean_USMA_edu_history

29
b

Once arriving at their assigned positions, each waited silently for the appointed hour. At midnight, they began crossing the swampy flanks to the south and north of the point. Finding themselves in water, at times two to four feet deep, the southern column took longer to reach the first of the obstructions or abatis. As they slogged thru the swamp, Wayne's men on the south and Murfree's diversionary force were fired upon by sentries who had spotted their advance.

As planned, Murfree's troops laid down a volley of fire, hoping to distract and draw attention toward them, in order that the flanking columns could reach the bastion, attracting as little attention as possible.

The diversion succeeded beyond the hopes of Washington and Wayne, drawing a counterattack. This response was made by half of the 625 man garrison, which consisted of the 17th Regiment of Foot, a grenadier company of the 71st Highlanders, and a strong detachment from the Loyal American Regiment. They were supported by artillery manned by members of the Royal Artillery. In retrospect, it would be difficult to imagine a more impregnable objective, commanded by more battle hardened troops. In addition, it was under the command of one of Clinton's most experienced officers, Lt. Col. Henry Johnston.

The British bayonet counterattack, carried out by six companies of the 17th Regiment, was stopped by Murfree and elements of the flanking forces, that cut off and blocked Johnston's withdrawal to the protection of the fort. Johnston and those surviving the counterattack were quickly captured leaving the British troops still inside the fortifications without an overall commander.

Pushing forward on the flanks, the brave men of the "forlorn hope" suffered horrendous losses but performed their duties successfully, allowing penetration of the fortifications on both flanks.

On the south flank, Wayne and his staff pushed forward, along with his troops, breaking through the first line of defenses. At the height of the battle, Wayne was struck in the forehead by a glancing blow from a spent musket ball. As Wayne began to topple from his horse, the alert Levan, who was riding beside him, reached out and was able to partially catch him as he fell to the ground.

Dazed but unfazed, Wayne rose to his knees and called out: "Forward, my brave fellows, forward." Quickly, Levan and his aides-de-camp were at his side. At first uncertain of the severity of the wound, Wayne ordered them, "Carry me into the fort, if I am to die, I want to die at the head of the column."

The scene is described by Levan in his Declaration:

> "Genl. Waine here received a slight wound. I was orderly to him and by him and catched him when like to fall."

Due to the stealth with which the American attack was carried out, they were upon the works, before the British could bring their artillery pieces to bear, in a manner successful enough to be of serious effect on the attackers.

The first men within the upper works were the Frenchman, de Fleruy, along with four noncommissioned officers, all who had received wounds in the early minutes of the assault. As they clambered into the works, they seized the British flag and Fleruy called out a prearranged alert: "The fort is ours." This was to indicate the capture of the fort and signal an end to British resistance.

With all of the columns breaching the fortifications at approximately the same time, and with Johnston and half of his garrison captured, the battle was over in less than half an hour. By 1 a.m., Stony Point was secure.

Despite his wound, Wayne joined in the celebration which erupted after the works were secure. It was clear to all, that what they had accomplished was of major significance. To Anthony Wayne, it was particularly satisfying, considering the similar humiliation he had endured at Paoli, almost two years previously. That defeat, although particularly stinging to Wayne, was insignificant in comparison to the losses suffered by the British at Stony Point. At Paoli, the American loss had been significant, primarily in human loss and in the brutal manner in which the British inflicted that loss. At Stony Point, the British had not only lost a strategic military position but the loss of an entire regiment and its commander. British losses were complete, with 543 prisoners taken including 74 wounded, while Wayne had lost but 15 men killed and 83 wounded. The number of British killed is uncertain, but a total number of those killed and missing would be in excess of sixty, based on the numbers reportedly manning the garrison.

That the attack was well planned and flawlessly executed is proven by the results. A further endorsement of the genius of the plan and execution comes from the insistence of the British commander, that he had not been taken by surprise and that each of his soldiers was at his post.

Despite what was undoubtedly a very painful wound, Wayne knew he must have the news carried to Washington. Following the celebration, he sat down to rest and to collect his thoughts. Seated near the point where the British flag had flown, Wayne looked around for his aides. Seeing Levan standing nearby, he recalled that he had come to his assistance and beckoned for him to approach.

"Soldier, I wanted to thank you for assisting me earlier. You may have saved me from further injury when you broke my fall. I am in your debt."

He then called out to his aides to provide him with paper and pen and he quickly composed a brief message to Washington.

Stony Point, 16 July 2 a.m.

Dear Gen'l.

The fort & garrison with Colonel Johnston are ours. Our officers & men behaved like men who are determined to be free.

Yours most sincerely

Ant'y Wayne

Once the letter had been written, Wayne sealed it and handed it to his aide, Captain Benjamin Fishbourn, with instructions to take the letter to General Washington and to take an escort with him.

"Captain, you are to ride to New Windsor, where I believe you will find General Washington and give him this message. Please relate to him as best you can what you have witnessed here tonight. Have this dragoon"—gesturing toward Levan—"and a couple more men accompany you for purposes of safety and to ensure the message reaches his excellency the general. If you need some rest, take a little time and then be on your way."

"Yes Sir," Fishbourn replied, saluting the general.

Fishbourn considered leaving at once, but aware that the ride of over twenty miles would be in darkness and would take two to three hours in good light, he thought better of leaving immediately. Finding a place in the garrison where they could rest the two men, along with two others who the captain had selected, determined to wait for better light before leaving. With their adrenalin rushing and not feeling particularly fatigued, despite the exertions of the march and the assault, the men were soon on their way to West Point.

In Levan's declaration, he speaks of his ride to West Point and the return.

> I was sent the same night to Genl. Washington with a express. He left fort Putnam immediately returned back with me to Genl. Waine.

Arriving at the point, the men were immediately taken to Washington, who was just finishing breakfast with his aides. Their conversation had centered on the prospects from the previous evening and the status of the rebuilding efforts on Fort Putnam and the other defenses at West Point.

Interrupting their conversation, Hamilton, who had been alerted to the arrival of messengers made their arrival known to the general.

"General Washington, sir. Beg your pardon for the interruption, but one of Wayne's aides and the young orderly Von Heer assigned to General Wayne are here with news from Stony Point," announced Hamilton.

"Well, for God's sakes bring them in," replied Washington. "Well, men, what news do you have for us?"

Withdrawing the dispatch from his pouch, Fishbourn handed it to Washington. "General Wayne has sent me to you with this message which I believe will explain everything," he exclaimed.

As Washington read the communication, an enormous smile came to his face and he quickly assembled his staff and joyfully read it aloud to all present. Elated by the news, Washington called for his horse to be saddled and ordered Hamilton to ready his staff and an escort for a return to Stony Point.

Turning toward Hamilton once again, he asked, "Can we get these men something to eat before they start back with me? I am sure they are famished, having had little time to eat anything since yesterday. I would like to get started as soon as they have been given that opportunity."

"Right away, General," Hamilton replied, as he quickly turned toward a pantry in the house where the general's cook was cleaning up from the morning meal.

Turning back toward Fishbourn and Levan, Washington once again addressed the captain and the young German.

"Get you something to eat while my horse is saddled and an escort assembled and meet us out in front as soon as you can. I would like to be on our way in ten or fifteen minutes."

The two men were quickly shown to a room where they were offered some sausages and biscuits and something to drink.

Washington quickly returned to his desk and hurriedly wrote a note to John Jay, who was serving as president of the Congress, and he ordered his aide Robert Harrison to inform General McDougall of the capture of Stony Point.

> Sir: I have the pleasure to transmit Your Excy the inclosed Copy of a Letter from Brigadier Genl. Wayne, which this moment came to hand. I congratulate Congress upon our success, and what makes it still more agreable from the report of Captn Fishbourn who brought me Genl. Wayne's Letter, the post was gained with but very inconsiderable loss on our part. As soon as I receive a particular account of the affair, I shall transmit it. I have the Honor, etc.

The letter to McDougall, in Harrison's handwriting, similarly informed the West Point commander of Wayne's success and it ordered him to send troops across the river to support a planned assault on Verplank' Point.

> Dr. Sir: I have the pleasure to inform you that Major Fishbourn has just arrived from Genl. Wayne, with the agreeable account of our having possessed ourselves of Stoney point and the whole Garrison with very little loss. You will throw the troops across the River, which I mentioned yesterday, with all possible expedition. I am, etc.

> P.S. You will order Nixon's Brigade to move immediately towards the Continl. Village. (Author's note: The Continental Village was a huge supply depot in the eastern Highlands near Fishkill, NY)

Levan and Fishbourn ate quickly and in little more than five minutes were out in front where Washington's staff and the escort were still assembling. A few minutes later, the party was on their way. Arriving at Stony Point in the early afternoon of July 16, they quickly sought out General Wayne.

They found Wayne busy securing the captured stores and seeing that the British prisoners were secured and readied to be marched away to confinement in Easton, Pennsylvania, a town north of Philadelphia and west of Morristown.

"General, I did not expect you so soon. Captain Fishbourn and the others certainly made good time," exclaimed Wayne.

"I am pleased to see you well. Levan told me of your wounding. How are you?"

"I am very well. It is nothing more than a scratch."

"General, I must offer you my most heartfelt congratulations on what is surely one of the finest military feats of our struggle. You and your men have surely exceeded my most liberal expectations of success," continued Washington. "I would like to address them if it is at all possible for you to assemble them in a place where I might offer my appreciation to them all."

"General, I fear it unlikely that all could be assembled in one place, but I will see that the officers and noncommissioned are gathered so that you may address them and as many of the others as is practicable."

"Very well," replied Washington. "That will be sufficient."

The assembly took place later in the day after the men finished securing prisoners and the captured stores. Washington heaped praise on the soldiers and offered his sincere appreciation for their bravery and the sacrifice of those killed and wounded.

The victory at Stony Point was a great moral boost for the long-suffering American forces, for the Congress and for the civilian population, who had been starved for a real victory since Saratoga almost two years before. Across the Hudson at Verplancks Point, a planned assault was abandoned after a cannonade from the captured guns at Stony Point did little damage to the defenses due to the distance involved. In addition, the force in place to carry out the assault was determined to have insufficient artillery needed for such an attack.

Washington was aware that to hold Stony Point, he would have to draw troops from West Point or Fort Montgomery and place those more strategic locations in peril; therefore, the fortifications at Stony Point were destroyed, and after securing the captured armaments and stores and exchanging the captured British officers, the post was abandoned on July 18.

The next day, General Clinton reoccupied Stony Point, only to abandon it prior to winter and concentrate his forces along the lower Hudson in what he felt was a better position to keep an eye on Washington. West Point would now be safe but for one last treacherous attempt to capture the fortress, through the treason of its commander, Benedict Arnold.

On July 21, Washington again wrote to the president of the Congress.

To the President of Congress

Head Quarters, New Windsor, July 21, 1779.

Sir: On the 16th instant, I had the honor to inform Congress of a successful attack upon the enemy's post at Stoney Point, on the preceding night, by Brigadier General Wayne and the corps of light infantry under his command. The ulterior operations in which we have been engaged, have hitherto put it out of my power to transmit the particulars of this interesting event. They will now be found in the inclosed report, which I have received from General Wayne. To the encomiums he has deservedly bestowed on the officers and men under his command, it gives me pleasure to add that his own conduct, throughout the whole of this arduous enterprise, merits the warmest approbation of Congress. He improved upon the plan recommended by me and executed it in a manner that does signal honor to his judgment and to his bravery. In a critical moment of the assault he received a flesh wound in the head with a musket-ball; but continued leading on his men with unshaken firmness.

With the victory at Stony Point, the major fighting in the northern theater of the war came to and end, and Clinton began to concentrate on a campaign in the south.

Levan rejoined the Provost and the unit moved south to New Jersey where they patrolled for the next few months, keeping a close eye on the British in New York City.

As the year came to a close, the Provost Company moved back north to New Windsor, a few miles from West Point, and the campaigning of 1779 came to and end.

In mid-October, Washington moved the majority of the main army to winter quarters at Jockey Hollow, near Morristown, New Jersey, with smaller bodies of troops scattered in the nearby New Jersey countryside and towns. The position at Jockey Hollow was strategic because it was situated on high ground several hundred feet above the British in New York, to the East, and located in an area where inhabitants were sympathetic to the American cause. The mountainous area also allowed Washington to keep up with any British movements and was a deterrent to any plan of attack by Clinton's forces.

On Christmas Day, 1779, Clinton, along with Lord Cornwallis, sailed for Savannah, Georgia, which had fallen the year before. His goal was to capture Charles Town, South Carolina, the leading port city in the southern colonies and to launch a campaign to win the war in the South. In doing so, he hoped to split the colonies in half, leaving the northern colonies to continue the fight on their own.

9

THE WAR TURNS SOUTH

THE WINTER THAT followed was the harshest of the war, with hardships exceeding the one at Valley Forge two years previously. Snow fell in record amounts, making roads impassable and the difficulties of supply for the hungry troops even greater. The troops suffered critical shortages of food, clothing, and blankets against the cold. Huts were constructed similar to those at Valley Forge, but even they could provide only so much protection from the elements.

Although the listed daily ration for an enlisted man was adequate, it was seldom available due to both the weather and funding from Congress. There were times when neither the listed issue of meat, flour, or vegetables was available and even days when nothing at all was issued.

The cold, poorly clothed, and unpaid men were not allowed to leave camp, fearing desertion, and worse, the concern that falling into British hands they might provide their captors with critical information about the circumstances of the American army.

The morale of the troops, both officers and enlisted men, suffered as a result of the support they received from their states and the Continental Congress, and their anger and resentment often boiled over into insubordination.

The encampment was marred by desertions and mutinies by some of the soldiers. Levan spoke of this in his declaration for pension:

> In the course of the winter the Pennsylvania troops rebelled and Washington sent to the Congress and the governor of Pennsylvania and the affair was settled......
> The latter the end of the winter the New Jersey troops rebelled also and by orders of Genl Washington, Genl. Howe took them. They were taken in Barnstown Plains. Two of the head ones was sentenced to be shot- the rest was put under Col. Barber where they had been in winter quarters.

The war, now soon to begin its sixth year, was at a stage never imagined by either side. The new American government was hardly equipped to handle peacetime, much less a war. The requirements of equipping and supplying an army of the size necessary to wage the war they now found themselves in were things never envisioned by the leaders of Congress. The most desperate situation was funding. The population was largely behind the new government, and the country was rich in natural resources but raising the resources to purchase what was needed was another question. The paper money issued was worthless and merchants and farmers were hesitant to accept the paper for their goods and services.

Meanwhile, in New York City, the British forces were well fed and comfortable even while the British loyalists among the population were pushing for action to be taken to end the war.

The main British army was relatively inactive during the winter months of early 1780, except for a few skirmishes between small groups foraging and probing the others lines. The loyalists in New York, on the other hand, found frequent opportunities to raid into rebel territories in New Jersey, particularly Elizabethtown and Newark.

In the South, however, it was an entirely different situation. Clinton had assembled a force of 14,000 soldiers and sailors for his drive on Charles Town. While bottling up the city from the sea, he landed his army to the south and advanced from John's Island, to James Island, just across the Ashley River. Crossing the river above the city, Clinton effectively cut off and began a siege that would last two months. The siege ended on May 12 with the American Commander Benjamin Lincoln, surrendering his 4,000 plus force and all military supplies. It was the worst defeat suffered by the American forces in terms of manpower and ordnance and allowed the British force to begin campaigns in the uplands of South Carolina. Clinton was now able to return to New York and turn his attention back to defeating Washington.

Finally as the spring thaw allowed more active military operations, the British began to formulate plans to move on the main American force at Morristown, and to end the war in the north once and for all.

In the last notable action in the New York area, the British under the Hessian General, Wilhelm von Knyphausen, who had commanded in Clinton's absence, attempted to regain control of northern New Jersey by launching an attack on the main Continental Army still encamped at Morristown. On June 7, his first push on the American forces was repulsed at the Battle of Connecticut Farms. Two weeks later, on June 23, a second British offensive was stopped by Nathanael Greene, in the Battle of Springfield. The two American victories ended British hopes to retake New Jersey and their ambitions to crush the Americans in the North.

Levan's declaration describes his role in the battles:

> I think in May we left Windsor and marched through
> Fishkill to Blanks (Verplanks) Point, here Washington
> commanded. Captain Colefax and lieutenant Cole with
> his life guard and 25 of the Marechausee or Van Heer's
> troops. I was one of them. We was sent to Maryseny
> (Mamaroneck) in Connecticut on the edge of New York.
> Hear we had a battle with a party of the Green Rangers
> and a part of the Hessian Riflemen commanded by Col.
> Wurmb. We took 30 or 40 of the Riflemen and killed
> several. We then returned back to Blanks (Verplanks)
> Pointe.

In the South, once Charles Town was secured, Cornwallis
began plans to move inland and to secure the rest of South
Carolina. Later that month, at Waxhaw, a group of soldiers from
Virginia, who had been sent to assist Lincoln at Charles Town,
were overtaken as they returned toward Virginia by Colonel
Banastre Tarleton of Cornwallis Cavalry. The Americans were
overwhelmed, and during an attempt to surrender, many who
had laid down their weapons were cut down by the British with
sabers. The brutal attack, provoked by a stray shot which had
taken down Tarleton's horse during the surrender, gave the
British a reason for retaliation on the men asking for quarter.
The incident resulted in the American's use of the battle cry
of "Tarleton's Quarter," which meant "Give no quarter." The
lingering resentment from this act resulted in many ongoing
acts of brutality between the British, their Loyalist allies, and
the rebels, in the dozens of battles and skirmishes throughout
South Carolina, during the remainder of the war in the South.

Two events occurred during August, leading to significant changes in the campaign for the Carolinas. In the first, the American cause suffered a major defeat at the Battle of Camden, where the recent congressionally appointed commander, Horatio Gates, blundered into battle against Cornwallis and Tarleton, with half of his force too ill with dysentery to fight. The battle resulted in the loss of half of Gates force and led to his being replaced by Nathanael Greene, a move which would reap benefits in later actions.

The second smaller scale event at Musgrove Mills resulted in an American victory over loyalist and provincial regulars and gave heart to the militia units operating in the backcountry.

Two months later, a thousand-man loyalist cavalry force, commanded by British Major Patrick Ferguson, would be surrounded by a militia force of equal size at Kings Mountain, in South Carolina. This band of frontiersmen was made up primarily of men from western Virginia, and the area that would become eastern Tennessee. These Over Mountain Men, as they came to be called, crushed Ferguson's force in a battle which resulted in the death of Ferguson and the capture of his entire force.

This victory was followed up with an equally significant result, only thirty miles away at a place called the Cowpens. Here Banastre Tarleton, Cornwallis's remaining cavalry commander, was lured into a brilliantly planned and executed trap. Here, the British commander was completely overwhelmed by an American force of militia and Continental troops commanded by the newly promoted General Daniel Morgan.

With the exception of a small contingent of cavalry escaping with Tarleton, the entire British force had once again been killed, wounded, or captured. The two victories are viewed by many as the turning point in the Revolution. The magnitude of the victories is reflected in the disparity in the losses. In the two battles, casualties for the Americans were 236 while the British losses are estimated at nearly 2,300.

These American victories rallied the people of the South and seeing no further course of action, Cornwallis began plans to move north. He hoped to intercept Daniel Morgan who he suspected would seek to rejoin Nathanael Greene near the Dan River, in upper North Carolina, near the Virginia border.

His expectation was that his recently reinforced army could prevent Morgan from joining Greene and that they could recover the 600 prisoners that Morgan had taken at the Cowpens. He also hoped at the same time to prevent Greene from returning to his supply bases north of the Dan in southern Virginia. To help him accomplish this ambitious plan and in order to maximize the speed of his movement, he ordered virtually his entire baggage train destroyed, including his personal belongings and those of his officers. Despite all his efforts, Morgan was able to reach Greene, and together they crossed the Dan, barely twelve hours before Cornwallis arrived.

Now safe, Greene could rest and resupply his army while Cornwallis pulled back to the south to Hillsboro where he camped and attempted to recruit loyalist to his army.

Once rested and resupplied, Greene crossed back into North Carolina, trying to determine a place to give battle to Cornwallis. Settling on Guilford Court House, Greene positioned his forces on high ground just south of the town and waited on Cornwallis to come to him.

His wait was short for Cornwallis's intelligence reports notified him of Greene's position and he quickly made plans to attack.

The battle, although brief, was at times very hotly engaged. Cornwallis, despite being outnumbered, was successful in forcing Greene to withdraw but with a cost of a quarter of his army. Many of the casualties resulted from friendly fire, as Cornwallis ordered his artillery to fire grape shot upon a hotly contested area of the battle, which he feared was going to turn in the American's favor. The decision broke the American surge but cost Cornwallis dearly in troops he could ill afford to lose.

Following the battle, Cornwallis moved his forces to the North Carolina coast at Wilmington, where he rested and resupplied his depleted army. At Wilmington, he was faced with some very difficult decisions. Chief among these would be the next move for his army. The lengthy campaigning had reduced his force to a size he felt incapable of performing the mission he had been given when placed in command in the South, but he had received nothing from Clinton to change those orders. While a period of continuous activity had existed in the Carolinas, a virtual stalemate had existed between Clinton and Washington, in New York, since the last British offensive had been repulsed at Connecticut Farms, the previous summer. Clinton had been raised in North America while his father was colonial governor of New York. He was in familiar surroundings in New York and virtually detached from any ongoing military activities and was very likely enjoying the dinner parties and other activities provided him by the rich loyalists of New York.

While at Wilmington, Cornwallis received dispatches informing him that two British forces had been sent to Virginia, one commanded by the traitor, Benedict Arnold, and the other by an old friend of Cornwallis, General William Phillips.

After a month in Wilmington, Cornwallis decided despite the orders that had limited him to the Carolinas, his best course of action was to join these two forces in Virginia and press the war there, hoping to achieve better results than he had in the Carolinas. His departure left Greene free to move his army back into South Carolina and, in a period of several months, to regain control of most of the State.

In late May, Cornwallis arrived in Petersburg, Virginia, to the news that Phillips had died only a few days before of fever.

Assuming command, he proceeded with the execution of the orders that Phillips had received from Clinton, to establish a naval station in southeast Virginia and, from that area, raid both military and civilian trade targets.

Opposing the British in the area was the Marquis de Lafayette, who was soon reinforced by Anthony Wayne. Despite the addition of Continental troops under Wayne, Lafayette's force, made up primarily of militia, was no match for that of Cornwallis, leading Lafayette to withdraw to the north toward his supply base at Fredericksburg.

After a short pursuit of Lafayette, Cornwallis gave up the chase and carried out his orders to establish the naval station and to harass targets of opportunity in the area southeast of Richmond.

By late summer, Cornwallis had chosen Yorktown as the site for his naval station and had begun to fortify the area, ceasing most other military operations in the area.

In June, a force of 5,000 French troops under General Comte de Rochambeau, left their base of operations at New Port, Rhode Island, and marched across Connecticut to join Washington, along the Hudson River north of New York. Rochambeau, despite his more extensive military career, offered his service and that of his troops, under Washington's overall command. Washington, whose army now outnumbered the British in New York by close to 3 to 1, considered an attack on the city and proposed his plan to the French general. Rochambeau was not in favor of the plan and convinced him that a movement south to join the French fleet under Comte de Grasse, sailing north from the West Indies to the Chesapeake, was preferable. Washington agreed and gave up plans for an attack on New York.

In mid-August, the two armies began a move south, followed ten days later by a French fleet under Comte de Barras, carrying additional troops, armaments, and siege equipment to support an attack on Cornwallis, at Yorktown.

Levan's declaration indicates that as the armies moved south, Washington employed Von Heer's mounted Dragoons as both body guard and escort and that he was often with those assigned to Washington.

From here, Washington took the company of Dragoons I was in…started before day lite and went to New Brunswick to breakfast and on to Trenton the same day by little after dark. Next morning we crossed the Delaware River before day light and on to Philadelphia to breakfast. Here we stayed several days till the army came up with us–then we marched to Wilmington stayed one night. Next day we moved to the Head of Elk and there stayed over a week till the artillery arrived and embarked from here Washington took the horsemen and we arrived at Baltimore the same day and met Genl. Lincoln. Here we was informed that Cornwallis was surrounded by a Genl. Greene by land and by Count De Grasse by water which was the cause of our rapid marching. We was marched from Baltimore to Alexandria from there to Fredericksburg, Virginia. Here we was musterd the second day by a Virginia major of the line. From there to Green Courthouse–from thence within 2 miles of Williamsburg. Here we stayed two or three days till Washington with his aide decamp came up with us he having went by horse. The same evening we was marched to headquarters and received orders to search the camps for the sick and take them to Williamsburg. The same night we followed the main army two or 3 miles and came up with them. We was then placed in front and continued in march all night. At the halfway house Major Nelson of the Va. state troops took the right hand road and we the left as the front guard of the French army. About day light we came up to the British picket guard in half a mile of Yorktown. Here we stayed till in the evening Washington reviewing the army with the horse with him. He then took up camp in an old field and set himself under a persimmon tree all night till the reveille late in the morning. He then with the horsemen with him went toward the town to spy out the situation of the enemy. He viewed with his spyglass and had like to have been killed by a cannonball passing his head—and took off both legs of a Maryland soldier. We then went to the French and was ordered to go 2 miles back towards Williamsburg to take up camp there. Washington took up his headquarters next the French Genl. Rochambeau.

In the weeks leading up to Washington's move south, confusion reigned at Yorktown. In mid-summer, Clinton, convinced that Washington was planning to attack New York, ordered Cornwallis to send what troops he could by ship to New York, to reinforce his position there. Learning later of Washington's move south, he rescinded that order and promised Cornwallis reinforcements, and he sent a Royal Fleet under Admiral Sir Thomas Graves, south to assist him. With the prospect of reinforcements and the impending arrival of Graves, Cornwallis decided to hold his position at Yorktown, instead of abandoning the fortifications and moving away, to avoid being surrounded by land and sea.

Unfortunately for Cornwallis, the reinforcements were not sent, and when Graves arrived off the Virginia coast, the first week of September, he was met by De Grasse, who had arrived the week before. The arrival of the French Fleet had trapped the British frigates assigned to Cornwallis and had prevented word of his situation reaching Clinton or Graves. De Grasse disembarked the 3,000 plus troops with him, and assigned ships to patrol the waters off the Cape. The French held a slight superiority in ships and armament and, after an off and on conflict lasting a week, were able to turn back Graves who immediately returned to New York. De Grasse, having been notified of the arrival of De Barras during this time, returned to the mouth of the Chesapeake to establish a blockade and assist in the siege of Yorktown.

Washington and Rochambeau arrived at nearby Williamsburg on September 14 and joined Lafayette and the French troops who had accompanied De Grasse. With the troops of De Grasse and the armaments and siege equipment brought by De Barras, Washington now had a formidable force of almost 20,000 troops.

Cornwallis was trapped.

During the next two weeks, Washington consolidated his forces and closed in on Yorktown, completing the envelopment on September 28. Realizing the nature of his situation, Cornwallis abandoned the outer redoubts and moved all his troops within the main fortifications. Washington immediately seized the abandoned positions and began to deploy artillery and to dig trenches. The bombardment began on the ninth, with Washington himself, firing the first cannon.

For the next five days, both the Americans and the French, kept up a continuous pounding of the British positions and, on the fourteenth, attacked and took the last remaining redoubts. From these new closer positions, the accuracy of the barrage improved and British casualties mounted. In one last attempt to avoid defeat, Cornwallis attempted to evacuate troops from Yorktown to his fortification at Gloucester Point, across the York River. This attempt was spoiled by a storm which scattered the boats and ended any remaining hope Cornwallis had of escaping.

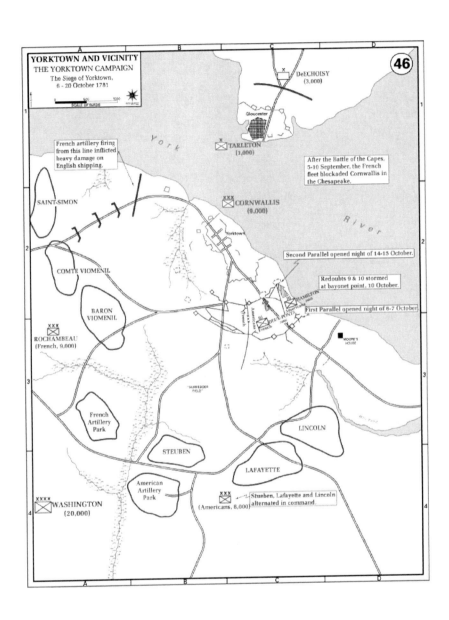

YORKTOWN AND VICINITY

THE YORKTOWN CAMPAIGN

The Siege of Yorktown,
6 - 20 October 1781

SCALE OF YARDS

46

DeECHOISY
(3,000)

Gloucester

French artillery firing
from this line inflicted
heavy damage on
English shipping.

York

TARLETON
(1,000)

After the Battle of the Capes,
5-10 September, the French
fleet blockaded Cornwallis in
the Chesapeake.

SAINT-SIMON

CORNWALLIS
(8,000)

River

COMTE VIOMENIL

Yorktown

Second Parallel opened night of 14-15 October.

Redoubts 9 & 10 stormed
at bayonet point, 10 October.

BARON
VIOMENIL

HAMILTON

First Parallel opened night of 6-7 October.

ROCHAMBEAU
(French, 9,000)

MOORE'S
HOUSE

"SURRENDER
FIELD"

French
Artillery
Park

LINCOLN

STEUBEN

American
Artillery
Park

LAFAYETTE

WASHINGTON
(20,000)

(Americans, 8,000) Steuben, Lafayette and Lincoln
alternated in command.

On the morning of the seventeenth, with all hope gone, the British commander sent out a drummer and an officer, with a white flag, seeking a cease fire, and the beginnings of a negotiated surrender. The next day, two representatives from each side met to work out the terms of surrender, and the following day, the British troops marched out of Yorktown and laid down their arms.

Cornwallis requested favorable terms of surrender similar to those given Burgoyne at Saratoga, but Washington refused his request, instead, imposing the same harsh conditions that Cornwallis had demanded of General Lincoln at Charles Town the year before. The war, for all intent and purposes, had come to a close.

In Levan's declaration for pension, he offers his recollection of the events at Yorktown.

> After our artillery landed the cannonading commenced and continued several days till the cessation of arms was made for three days. Cornwallis there surrendered and in a few days afterward the enemy marched out. We the horsemen was put in charge of the Dutch prisoners and marched with them to Frederick Town in Maryland and there left the prisoners in care of the militia and from there went to a place called Carlise in Pennsylvania.

In the months following, Lord North resigned as British prime minister and British troops were withdrawn from Savannah and Charleston.

Articles of Peace were signed a year later in November 1782, and the treaty ratified by Congress in April of the next year. On September 2, 1783, the formal treaty was signed in Paris, and in

November, the last of the British troops in America, left New York. Eight years of war were at an end.

Levan's service continued after Yorktown, as he reenlisted once again in March of 1782. His declaration describes escort service for Washington, along with other members of the Provost Guard and his personal service as an orderly in Washington's headquarters, often at Newburg, New York.

On June 23, 1783, Isaac Levan was discharged for the last time from the service of the United States. He had served his newly adopted country for eight years and three months. Like so many others, some whose names are well-known and others whose identities were lost to time, he had played a role in the formation of what became the greatest bastion of freedom in the world.

EPILOGUE

THE LATER YEARS

SOON AFTER BEING discharged from service in June 1783, Levan returned to Philadelphia, where he lived until 1785. In that year, he traveled by foot to the Catawba River area of North Carolina, where he settled. It is likely that Levan traveled to the area with others of German descent, as history records that many who settled in North Carolina, after the Revolution were of German ancestry.

According to Lincoln County, North Carolina, marriage records, he married a Mary Rosimond on February 5, 1789. Census records for 1790 show two males under sixteen and four total females in his household. This could indicate that either he or Mary had been married previously and had children from the prior marriage. Census records for 1810 show six males and six females in the Levan household.

Although he had been promised 160 acres of land each time he enlisted, Levan had never received the benefits of these promises. In 1832, he made a declaration before the court of Burke County, North Carolina, seeking to obtain the benefit of the provisions made by an Act of Congress passed June the 7, 1832. This act provided that every officer or enlisted man who had served at least two years in the Continental Line or State troops, volunteers or militia, was eligible for a pension of full pay for life. His declaration was apparently set aside for lack of proper documentation. His file, at the national archives, contains numerous letters written on his behalf and includes correspondence from those in Washington, who reviewed his request, stating the reasons for their refusal of his petition. It is clear from the detailed information in his declaration and the verification in later years, from men who served with him and others who remembered his service, that he did indeed serve in the units he mentioned. His failure to keep his discharge papers over the nearly fifty-year period, between his service and his declaration and the lack of the surviving muster rolls placing him in those companies, appear to be the only reason he was denied the pension he so richly deserved.

Levan continued to live in the Catawba River area until his death in January 1850. Census records taken that same month list him as a resident of a pauper's home.

Based on the mortality records of that year, it appears that Levan had earned his living as a schoolteacher. Sadly, they indicate that he froze to death in the home for the poor, where he lived at the end of his life.

Declaration

In order to obtain the benefit of the Act of Congress of the 7th of June 1832 State of North Carolina Burke County.

On this 24th of January 1837 personally appeared Isaac Levan aged near 79 years and after being duly sworn according to law, doth on his oath make the following declaration in order to obtain the benefit of the provisions made by the Act of Congress passed June the 7th 1832. That he enlisted in the army of the United States on the 3rd day of March in the year 1775 under Captain Sealy (Captain Anthony Selin) and served in what was called the Dutch Battalion commanded by Major Dechert. Afterwards the name of the Dutch Battalion was the Congress Regiment. Changed its name I think in the spring of 1777 and commanded by General Hazen. (Regiment also known as Congress' Own or Hazen's Regiment) I still served as a private under Captain Sealy and served three years in that capacity. I think my Lieutenants name was Docky or Ducky. The name of the Ensign I have forgotten. He was a French man.

My mess mates was George Brieger, Henry Fleisher, and John Mininger, Michael Stoner, Jacob Frey, Conrad Sitler.

I lived in Philadelphia when I listed and marched from there on the 5th day on our way to Fort Edward in New York and there joined Col. Proctors Artillery. Stayed there two days and then marched to Lake George to the Fort high on the rock (most likely Fort George) and there on the 8th day of May we had battle with the British. We had joined Gen. Sullivan and Gen. Montgomery's army. We with a few of the New England volunteers commanded by Gen. Arnold, left the main army crossed Lake George and the St. Lawrence and marched to a town called the Three Rivers and stayed there about six weeks and then marched down towards Quebec and met the main army on Abrahams Plains and had battle with the enemy on the 31st day of December 1775 in which Gen. Montgomery was killed. We then left there and went to guard the Little River at Wolf's Cove to keep the British from coming up the river. Six or seven British boats came up, we fired a few rounds at them. They retreated from thence we was ordered back to Crown Point from then to Chimney Point to keep the enemy from going over to Vermont. We took our winter quarters there and stayed till in May and then marched to Fort Edward from thence to Albany.

From there to work in New York and there joined General Washington's army and the winter of 1776 was spent without having one settled place for winter quarters as the British was at Brunswick and Little Amboy and Elizabeth Town point so that we had to shift to guard them as we could. No battle only one little skirmish in April. We left there and followed after the enemy towards Burlington and General Lee commanded the 2nd Division that I was in and he left his Division at a creek and went to a tavern called Whites Tavern near Lord Sterling's buildings (referring to the home of Continental General William Alexander, Lord Sterling) and was there taken prisoner by 5 or 6 British Dragoons. From there we followed after the enemy back to Amboy and Woodbridge and stayed about three weeks in Amboy and the enemy on Staten Island. We then left there to Newtons thence to Cooche's ferry in Delaware from thence to Head of Elk. Stayed 2 or 3 weeks from thence to Brandywine and had a battle on 11th day of September 1777. From thence to Paoli, there the enemy came on the men commanded by General Waine (Anthony Wayne) in the night and killed 600 of them by the bayonet. From thence we went to Germantown and there had a battle on the 11th day of October (actually the 2nd). We had to retreat from the enemy but continued about

White Marsh 5 or 6 weeks. The enemy came on us at White Marsh and we had another engagement. We drove them back and from there we went to winter quarters with Col. Nagles Regt. to the brick meeting house nine miles from Philadelphia. We had been reviewed in Valley Forge by General Miflin in November or December before we went to winter quarters.

In June we left there, relieved by the Pennsylvania militia. Crossed the Delaware River at Easton and then went to Minisink then to Boundbrook from there to Monmouth and there we had a battle with the enemy on the 24th of June 1778. In this battle both armies retreated. General Lee commanded the left wing and gave orders to retreat wrongfully as the enemy was retreating at the same time. From there we marched to the state of Connecticut and stayed in Fredericksburg till in November and then went to Middlebrook and Boundbrook. Washington had his headquarters on Raritan River. The Pennsylvanians had theirs between ? river and Millstone River. Here I was discharged on the third day of March 17th 1779 by Captain Sealy by order of General Hazen. I then enlisted again the same day after my discharge a Dragoon for three years more under Capt Bartholomew Van Heer. The regiment was called Marechausee. The first lieutenant was Phillip Manke–the second lieutenant was Jacob Menninger–the coronet was Baron Wolfin. We had no Col. over us only as they was appointed at different times to muster us. The first of them was Col. Stuart of the second regiment of the Pennsylvania troops in the town of Redding—while in winter quarters. We marched from Raritan River in the spring of 1779 in April or May to Smith's Clove. Washington that his headquarters there by Smith's Tavern. From here we was sent down Smith's river five miles to General Sinclair as a front guard of the army. Stayed about three weeks then marched over the mountains to west point on north river.

Here we built two forts. The one next the river was called Putnam the other was on the hill (in fact Fort Putnam was on the hill and Fort Clinton next to the river). Here we put in the river a Chevaux-Defrise. At this place we had to patrol from fort Putnam to Stony Point every day til General Waine took the fort at Stony Point in July 1779. General Waine here received a slight wound. I was orderly to him and by him and catched him when like to fall. I was sent the same night to General Washington with a express. He left fort Putnam immediately returned back with me to General Waine. Stayed one day and the next day we destroyed the fort and the British Rogueally (Row Gally). Then we marched to Depon. Here we stayed about two months with the whole army and then left there and went to the English neighborhood and Washington to Doday's bridge. Here we had to patrol down to the *three Peacheys*. From here we marched to New Windsor in New York to winter quarters. General Waine and Smallwood took up theirs seven miles from Morristown at *seven peaceys*. The light horse theirs in little Britain. General Knox with the artillery theirs at *Pluckimen*. In the course of the winter the Pennsylvania troops rebelled and Washington sent to the Congress and the governor of Pennsylvania and the affair was settled. The regiments was divided and in the spring they were sent to General Greene in the south. The latter the end of the winter the New Jersey troops rebelled also and by orders of General Washington, General Howe took them. They were taken in Barnstown Plains. Two of the head ones was sentenced to be shot- the rest was put under Col. Barber where they had been in winter quarters. I think in May we left Windsor and marched through Fishkill to Blanks (Verplanks) Point, here Washington commanded. Captain Colefax and lieutenant Cole with his life guard and 25 of the Marechausee or Van Heer's troops. I was one of them.

We was sent to Maryseny (Mamaroneck) in Connecticut on the edge of New York. Hear we had a battle with a party of the Green Rangers and a part of the Hessian Riflemen commanded by Col. Wurmb. We took 30 or 40 of the Riflemen and killed several. We then returned back to Blanks (Verplanks) Pointe then Washington removed his headquarters to Anderson's Point from hear(sic) the Light Horse was sent to Hackensack against the refugees that was taking some of the people while they was moving their meadows but they was gone. We took none of them. We returned to Washington again. The next day he marched the army off, crossed the North River at Kings Ferry, stayed 2 nights at the white house waiting for the Rhode Island Regiment and the balance of the Army and the French Army. From here, Washington took the company of Dragoons I was in...started before day lite and went to New Brunswick to breakfast and on to Trenton the same day by little after dark. Next morning we crossed the Delaware River before day light and on to Philadelphia to breakfast. Here we stayed several days till the army came up with us–then we marched to Wilmington stayed one night. Next day we moved to the Head of Elk and there stayed over a week till the artillery arrived and embarked from here Washington took the horsemen and we arrived at Baltimore the same day and met General Lincoln. Here we was informed that Cornwallis was surrounded by a General Greene by land and by Count De Grasse by water which was the cause of our rapid marching. We was marched from Baltimore to Alexandria from there to Fredericksburg, Virginia. Here we was musterd the second day by a Virginia major of the line. From there to Green Courthouse–from thence within 2 miles of Williamsburg. Here we stayed two or three days till Washington with his aide decamp came up with us he having went by horse. The same evening we was marched to headquarters and received orders to search the camps for the sick and take them to Williamsburg. The same night we followed the main army two or 3 miles and came up with them. We was then placed in front and continued in march all night. At the halfway house Major Nelson of the Va. state troops took the right hand road and we the left as the front guard of the French army. About day light we came up to the British picket guard in half a mile of Yorktown. Here we stayed till in the evening Washington reviewing the army with the horse with him. He then took up camp in an old field and set himself under a persimmon tree all night till the reveille late in the morning. He then with the horsemen with him went toward the town to spy out the situation of the enemy. He viewed with his spyglass and had like to have been killed by a cannonball passing his head—and took off both legs of a Maryland soldier. We then went to the French and was ordered to go 2 miles back towards Williamsburg to take up camp there. Washington took up his headquarters next the French General Rochambeau. Col. Scammell of the grenadiers took a party of men and went to storm the redoubt and got wounded and was taken prisoner and was run so hard he bled to death. After our artillery landed the cannonading commenced and continued several days till the cessation of arms was made for three days. Cornwallis there surrendered and in a few days afterward the enemy marched out. We the horsemen was put in charge of the Dutch prisoners and marched with them to Frederick Town in Maryland and there left the prisoners in care of the militia and from there went to a place called Carlise in Pennsylvania. There we stayed in winter quarters. In March my three years expired and I was discharged sometime in March 1782. I then took the bounty again and listed for during the war under Captain Bartholomew Van Heer. Jacob Minniger was first Lt. Philip Stuban was 2nd Lt., John Stake was Coronet, one Obrian was clerk of the Company. Our Lieutenant Minniger and 25 Dragoons, I was one of them, and one sergeant one corporal and trumpeter was ordered to march to Philadelphia and there we met with General Washington and marched with him to Newberg in New York State and took up quarters till the French army came to us. We then crossed north river and went to Blanks (Verplanks) Point. At this place the main northern army joined us again. We stayed there till the end of November. We went to winter quarters. The light horse to Goshen till in February and then went to the Drowned lands (likely near New Windsor) was mustered by Maj. Barber there. Washington stayed in Newberg and in March near the last General Howe broke the news from Boston that peace was made. I was a orderly in headquarters then and was sent with him to Barnstown plains to General Hazen. I returned and then we went to Oldpaltz on the river Wallkill and remained there till the 23rd day of June 1783. Then Maj. Barber aide decamp to the muster master general mustered us and on calling over the list give us our discharges in print and dismissed us June the 23 1783.

—Isaac Levan

I Isaac Levan hereby relinquishes every claim whatsoever to a pension or annuity except the present and declares that his name is not on the Pension Roll of the agency of any state or if any only on that of the agency of North Carolina.

—Isaac Levan

The Provost Guard

Trooper
Von Heer's
Provost Corps
1778 - 1783

The Military Police Corps of today traces its early stages to a provost unit, sometimes referred to as the Marechaussee Corps, in the Continental Army.

As early as June 1775, upon assuming command, General George Washington discovered the lack of military discipline evidenced in the newly formed American army. Most officers, lacking military training, were reluctant to give orders, and orders given were often disobeyed or ignored.

Drunkenness, thieving, straggling, and desertion were common. There was little control with regard to the security of the camp, leading to infiltration by unscrupulous settlers, civilian visitors, both suitable and unsuitable, the unsuitable including prostitutes and spies. In addition, there was no provision for the disciplining of soldiers found guilty of misconduct or the handling of British prisoners captured during battle.

In November of 1777, Washington received a letter from an officer serving in the Pennsylvania Continental Line.

Bartholomew Von Heer had served in the army's of Prussia, France, and Spain before immigrating to America to join the American forces and was familiar with the military guards or provost of those countries. He offered his services in equipping and training such a force for the Continental Army if he would be given command.

In January of 1778, Washington called for a reorganization of the Continental Army and the establishment of a Provost Corps within that reorganization. Washington desired men of this new Corp to be dependable above all else, and in return, they would receive higher pay. They would be charged with "watching over the good order and regularity of the army." The recommendations of Von Heer were that the Corps be drafted from the brigades and be mounted and armed and accoutered as light dragoons.

On May 20, 1778, the Continental Congress passed the resolution which formed a permanent Provost Corps. On June 6, 1778, orders were issued for the establishment of the new Provost Corps made up of the following: there were to be sixty-three men and they were to be armed, uniformed, and accoutered as light dragoons. In addition to Von Heer, there were four lieutenants, one quartermaster sergeant, and one clerk. The Corps was divided into two troops with a trumpeter, a sergeant, and five corporals assigned to each troop. There were forty-three dragoons and four executioners. Their uniform would be blue coats with yellow facings and vests, leather breeches, and a visored leather helmet typical of those worn by light dragoons. They were to be a mounted unit, as Von Heer had suggested, allowing them the mobility and speed required to carry out their mission.

Von Heer began recruitment in June, 1778 with little success, due to the stigma accompanying the duties of the provost, until it was proposed that those men joining the provost for a period of three years, or the duration of the war, would receive both the state bounty and the Continental bounty. This inducement coupled with Von Heer's targeting the German-speaking areas, between Reading, and Philadelphia, soon allowed for the completion of the complement of the Corp.

During its five years of existence, Von Heer's Marechaussee Corps served the Continental Army with distinction. They often acted as an honor guard and periodically as a body guard for the commanding general, when the infantry unit assigned as his life guard, was limited by being dismounted. Small groups of the unit were also often assigned, at the request of Washington, to serve as couriers and aides to both himself and to other general officers in the army.

The Marechausee has the distinction to be one of the last units discharged from the Continental Army after hostilities had ceased.

Exhibit I
The Boston Tea Party

The Boston Tea Party was a direct action by colonists in Boston, a town in the British colony of Massachusetts, against the British government. On December 16, 1773, after officials in Boston refused to return three shiploads of taxed tea to Britain, a group of colonists boarded the ships and destroyed the tea by throwing it into Boston Harbor. The incident remains an iconic event of American history, and reference is often made to it in other political protests.

The Tea Party was the culmination of a resistance movement throughout British America, against the Tea Act, which had been passed by the British Parliament in 1773. Colonists objected to the Tea Act, for a variety of reasons, especially because they believed that it violated their right to be taxed only by their own elected representatives. Protesters had successfully prevented the unloading of taxed tea in three other colonies, but in Boston, embattled Royal Governor Thomas Hutchinson refused to allow the tea to be returned to Britain. He apparently did not expect that the protestors would choose to destroy the tea rather than concede the authority of a legislature in which they were not directly represented.

The Boston Tea Party was a key event in the growth of the American Revolution. Parliament responded in 1774 with the Coercive Acts, which, among other provisions, closed Boston's commerce until the British East India Company had been repaid for the destroyed tea. Colonists, in turn, responded to the Coercive Acts with additional acts of protest, and by convening the First Continental Congress, which petitioned the

British monarch for repeal of the acts and coordinated colonial resistance to them. The crisis escalated, and the American Revolutionary War began near Boston in 1775.

Exhibit II
The Intolerable Acts

The Boston Port Act, the first of the acts passed in response to the Boston Tea Party, closed the port of Boston until the East India Company had been repaid for the destroyed tea and until the king was satisfied that order had been restored. Colonists objected that the Port Act punished all of Boston, rather than just the individuals who had destroyed the tea, and that they were being punished without having been given an opportunity to testify in their own defense.

The Massachusetts Government Act created even more outrage than the Port Act because it unilaterally altered the government of Massachusetts, to bring it under control of the British government. Under the terms of the Government Act, almost all positions in the colonial government were to be appointed by the governor or the king. The act also severely limited the activities of town meetings in Massachusetts. Colonists outside Massachusetts feared that their governments could now also be changed by the legislative fiat of Parliament.

The Administration of Justice Act allowed the governor to move trials of accused royal officials to another colony or even to Great Britain if he believed the official could not get a fair trial in Massachusetts. Although the act stipulated that witnesses would be paid for their travel expenses, in practice, few colonists could afford to leave their work and cross the ocean to testify in a trial. George Washington called this the Murder Act because he believed that it allowed British officials to harass Americans and then to escape justice. Some colonists believed the act was unnecessary because British soldiers had been given a fair trial following the Boston Massacre in 1770.

The Quartering Act applied to all of the colonies and sought to create a more effective method of housing British troops in America. In a previous act, the colonies had been required to provide housing for soldiers, but colonial legislatures had been uncooperative in doing so. The new Quartering Act allowed a governor to house soldiers in other buildings if suitable quarters were not provided. While many sources claim that the Quartering Act allowed troops to be billeted in occupied private homes, historian David Ammerman's 1974 study claimed that this is a myth and that the act only permitted troops to be quartered in unoccupied buildings. Although many colonists found the Quartering Act objectionable, it generated the least protest of the Intolerable Acts.

The Quebec Act was a piece of legislation unrelated to the events in Boston, but the timing of its passage led it to be labeled as one of the Intolerable Acts. The act enlarged the boundaries of the Province of Quebec and instituted reforms generally favorable to the French Catholic inhabitants of the region, although denying them an elected legislative assembly. The Quebec Act offended a variety of interest groups in the British colonies. Land speculators and settlers objected to the transfer of western lands previously claimed by the colonies to a non-representative government. Many feared the establishment of Catholicism in Quebec, and that the French Canadians were being courted to help oppress Americans.

Exhibit III
First Continental Congress

The First Continental Congress was a convention of delegates, from twelve of the thirteen North American colonies, that met on September 5, 1774, at Carpenters' Hall, in Philadelphia, Pennsylvania, early in the American Revolution. Called in response to the passage of the Coercive Acts, (also known as Intolerable Acts by the Colonial Americans) by the British Parliament, the Congress was attended by fifty-six members who had been appointed by the legislatures of twelve, of the Thirteen Colonies, the exception being the Province of Georgia, which did not send delegates. At the time, Georgia was the newest and smallest province and declined to send a delegation because it was seeking help from London, in pacifying its smoldering Indian frontier.

The Congress met briefly to consider options, including an economic boycott of British trade, to publish a list of rights and grievances, and to petition King George for redress of those grievances.

The Congress also called for another Continental Congress in the event that their petition was unsuccessful in halting enforcement of the Intolerable Acts. Their appeal to the Crown had no effect; therefore, the Second Continental Congress was convened the following year, to organize the defense of the colonies, at the onset of the American Revolutionary War. The delegates also urged each colony to set up and train its own militia.

The Congress met from September 5 to October 26, 1774. From September 5 through October 21, Peyton Randolph presided over the proceedings; Henry Middleton took over as president of the Congress for the last few days, from the twenty-second of October to the twenty-sixth of October.

Charles Thomson, leader of Philadelphia Sons of Liberty, was selected to be secretary of the Continental Congress.

Patrick Henry already considered the government dissolved and was seeking a new system. Pennsylvania delegate Joseph Galloway sought reconciliation with Britain. He put forth a Plan of Union, which suggested that an American legislative body be formed, that held some authority, and whose consent would be required for imperial measures. John Jay, Edward Rutledge, and other conservatives supported Galloway's plan. (Galloway would later join the Loyalists).

The Congress had two primary accomplishments. The first was a compact among the colonies to boycott British goods, beginning on December 1, 1774. The West Indies were threatened with a boycott unless the islands agreed to nonimportation of British goods. Imports from Britain dropped by 97 percent in 1775 compared with the previous year. Committees of observation and inspection were to be formed in each colony for enforcement of the Association. All of the colonial Houses of Assembly approved the proceedings of the Congress with the exception of New York.

If the Intolerable Acts were not repealed, the colonies would also cease exports to Britain after September 10, 1775. The boycott was successfully implemented, but its potential for altering British colonial policy was cut off by the outbreak of the American Revolutionary War.

The second accomplishment of the Congress was to provide for a Second Continental Congress to meet on May 10, 1775. In addition to the colonies which had sent delegates to the First Continental Congress, letters of invitation were sent to Quebec (three letters), Saint John's Island, Nova Scotia, Georgia, East

Florida, and West Florida. None of these sent delegates to the opening of the second Congress, though a delegation from Georgia, arrived the following July.

Exhibit IV
The Battles of Lexington and Concord

By the beginning of 1775, the British government had become increasingly concerned about the growing number of militias, and on April 14, 1775, General Thomas Gage, commander of the British forces in Boston, and the military governor of Massachusetts, received instructions to disarm the rebels, confiscate weapons hidden in Concord, and to imprison the rebellion's leaders.

On the morning of April 18, Major Mitchell of the 5th Regiment of Foot was ordered to take a mounted patrol out into the countryside to intercept any messages intended to warn the militia of British movements. That same afternoon, Lieutenant Colonel Francis Smith received sealed orders from Gage to march out of Boston toward Concord, opening those orders once the march was underway. He was to proceed to Concord and seize and destroy all military stores. He was also directed to take care that the soldiers did not harm or plunder the inhabitants or destroy private property. Gage, fearing the worst, used his discretion and withheld any orders calling for the arrest of rebel leaders.

The rebel leaders had received word of the crown's instructions to Gage from sources in London even before they had reached the general himself. They had also been notified of the details of the British plans for the eighteenth through the efforts of William Dawes and Paul Revere, who had ridden out from Boston, at the direction of Dr. Joseph Warren, president of the Massachusetts Provincial Congress. Their efforts spread the word of the impending British expedition to Concord and Lexington. It is suspected that the source of this intelligence was the New Jersey-born wife of General Gage, whose sympathies were with the Colonial cause and who was a friend of Dr. Warren.

As a result of the forewarning, the stock of weapons, powder, and supplies at Concord and at Worcester were removed and the stores distributed among other nearby towns.

The British embarked in boats from Boston, bound for Cambridge around 11 p.m. on the night of April 18 and disembarked in Cambridge into waist-deep water at midnight. By the time all were disembarked and their gear unloaded, the British regulars began their march toward Concord at about 2 a.m. As they marched, officers aware of their mission realized from the sounds of colonial alarms throughout the countryside that they would not be a surprise to the militia members.

The British advance guard, commanded by Major Pitcairn, entered Lexington about sunrise, immediately being confronted by Lexington militiamen, led by Captain John Parker, a veteran of the French and Indian War. The men emerged from Buckman Tavern and formed ranks on the village common. Parker is reported to have ordered his men to "stand your ground; don't fire unless fired upon, but if they mean to have a war, let it begin here," a statement that is now engraved in stone at the site of the battle. The following is from a sworn deposition by Parker taken after the battle:

> I ordered our Militia to meet on the Common in said Lexington to consult what to do, and concluded not to be discovered, nor meddle or make with said Regular Troops (if they should approach) unless they should insult or molest us; and, upon their sudden Approach, I immediately ordered our Militia to disperse, and not to fire:—Immediately said Troops made their appearance and rushed furiously, fired upon, and killed eight of our

Party without receiving any Provocation therefore from us.

The militia men were ordered by a British officer to disperse and to lay down their arms. Captain Parker told his men instead to disperse and go home, with no order to give up their arms. As many of the militia members withdrew, a shot was fired from an unknown source and the British fired upon the assembled crowd.

Lieutenant John Barker, of the 4th Regiment of Foot recalled the incident in the following statement:

> At 5 o'clock we arrived, and saw a number of people, I believe between 200 and 300, formed in a common in the middle of town; we still continued advancing, keeping prepared against an attack through without intending to attack them; but on our coming near them they fired on us two shots, upon which our men without any orders, rushed upon them, fired and put them to flight; several of them were killed, we could not tell how many, because they were behind walls and into the woods. We had a man of the 10th light Infantry wounded, nobody else was hurt. We then formed on the Common, but with some difficulty, the men were so wild they could hear no orders; we waited a considerable time there, and at length proceeded our way to Concord.

Some reported that the first shot was fired by a colonial from near the tavern and others reported it came from within the British lines. It is impossible to determine, with any certainty, which side fired the shot which began the American Revolution.

The battle at Lexington lasted only a few minutes and left eight colonials dead and ten wounded. Only one British soldier was wounded. One of the wounded colonials, Prince Estabrook was a black slave who was serving in the militia.

Colonel Smith arrived shortly after the eruption of firing along with the grenadiers and restored order among his troops. He reformed the column and resumed the march toward Concord where militia was now assembling. Initially outnumbered by the advancing British, the militiamen retreated from Concord and assembled on a hill across the North Bridge and about a mile north of town where their numbers continued to grow.

Upon arriving in Concord and securing both the North and South bridges leading from town, the British began their search for military supplies, both in the town and on neighboring farms. Their search yielded little of significance other than three massive twenty-four-pound cannons, which the British rendered useless.

Upon the arrival of additional men, the militia, commanded by Colonel James Barrett, moved off their vantage point atop the hill and advanced on the North Bridge, forcing the British troops at the foot of the hill to retreat to the Bridge.

As the militia, outnumbering the British about 40 to 1, advanced in column formation, the British retreated across the bridge and formed a line of battle which proved useless against the militia formed in column. As at Lexington, an unordered shot was fired leading to other shots and eventually a volley from the British line, which killed two militiamen instantly. The opposing Forces, now separated only by the Concord River and the bridge some fifty yards across, quickly were locked in combat. A returned volley by the militia killed and wounded approximately a dozen of the British troops, forcing the outnumbered British to abandon their wounded and retreat back toward town approaching grenadiers.

The colonists resumed a defensive position, observing that the British in Concord, were rejoined by a detachment of regulars, who had been sent to search a local farm. After all the British forces had returned to Concord, they ate, reassembled for marching, and left Concord in the early afternoon, their delay allowing time for additional militia to assemble along the road back to Boston.

As the British retreated along the road back to Boston, they were harassed by firing, coming from the cover of trees, rocks, and fences. The militia, now numbering 2,000, continued to beleaguer the British column until it was finally reinforced and eventually reached Charlestown in midafternoon.

The day's fighting had cost the militia fifty killed, thirty-nine wounded, and five missing. The march had profited the British little but to enflame the Colonist further and cost them 73 killed, 173 wounded, and 26 missing.

The next morning, General Gage found himself surrounded by a huge militia army, numbering in excess of 15,000 which had rushed to Boston, from throughout New England.

The battle, not major in terms of tactics or casualties, was nonetheless significant because the expedition contributed to the hostility it was intended to prevent and only further enflamed the rebellious feeling in the Colonies and truly began the Revolutionary War.

The militia army continued to swell as men and supplies arrived from the surrounding colonies. Eventually, many of these men were adopted into the beginnings of the Continental Army, and two months later, the armies would clash at Breed and Bunker Hills. Eventually, Washington would take command of the forces surrounding Boston, forcing the British to abandon Boston and occupy New York City.